Big 'n Easy

Big 'n Easy

Supersized Quilts for Queen Beds

Judy Hopkins

Martingale®
& COMPANY

JW

Big 'n Easy: Supersized Quilts for Queen Beds
© 2005 by Judy Hopkins

That Patchwork Place® is an
imprint of Martingale & Company®.

Martingale & Company
20205 144th Avenue NE
Woodinville, WA 98072-8478 USA
www.martingale-pub.com

Printed in China
10 09 08 07 06 05   8 7 6 5 4 3 2 1

Mission Statement

Dedicated to providing quality products
and service to inspire creativity.

Credits

President: Nancy J. Martin
CEO: Daniel J. Martin
VP and General Manager: Tom Wierzbicki
Publisher: Jane Hamada
Editorial Director: Mary V. Green
Managing Editor: Tina Cook
Technical Editor: Laurie Baker
Copy Editor: Melissa Bryan
Design Director: Stan Green
Illustrator: Robin Strobel
Cover Designer: Stan Green
Text Designer: Regina Girard
Photographer: Brent Kane

Library of Congress Cataloging-in-Publication Data
Hopkins, Judy.
  Big 'n Easy : supersized quilts for queen beds / Judy
Hopkins.
    p. cm.
  ISBN 1-56477-550-X
 1. Patchwork—Patterns. 2. Quilting. 3. Patchwork
quilts. I. Title.
  TT835.H5584 2005
  746.46'041—dc22
                                    2005016003

Dedication

In loving memory of Trish Delong

Your absence has gone through me
Like thread through a needle.
Everything I do is stitched with its color.
—W. S. Merwin, "Separation"

Acknowledgments

Special thanks, as always, to the quiltmakers, the quilters, the pattern testers, and the photographer's assistants—some of whom wore more than one hat! They are: Jaxine Andersen, Clare Brooks, Craig "Grumpy" Campbell, Rianne Campbell, Jackie Carley, Sandi Carr, Mary Daly, Judy DeLano, Anne Derting, Tracey Dukowitz, Nancy Goldsworthy, Janet Gorton, JoAnn Gruber, Michelle Gwin, Michele Hall, Connie Hanser, Amy Helmkamp, Linda Humfeld, Judy Irish, Sarah Kaufman, Julie Kimberlin, Marianne McCabe, Judy Morley, Martha Morris, Kathy Mosher, Janet Murdock, Mona Norris, Nellie Oldaker, Kay Oft, Carol Parks, Clare St. Sure, Ann Schoblaske, Beverly Schutt, Sue Scott, Terri Shinn, Deanna Smith, Juanita Stark, Donna Stevenson, Ann Symons, Kathy White, Joanne Wilder, and Chris Winter.

Thanks also to Marsha McCloskey and Clothworks/Fasco Fabric Sales Company for the Staples fabrics used in "Double Nine Patch," and to Susan Baxter of Fanno Creek Calicos for providing introductions to terrific people and access to convenient work and meeting space.

Contents

9 Introduction

11 Basic Quiltmaking Instructions

Projects

15 Around the Block

19 Bars

21 Basket Weave

24 Blocks in a Box

26 Burgoyne Surrounded

31 Cornucopia

34 Checkers

37 Courthouse Stars

42 Double Nine Patch

45 Far West

50 Four Square

53 Grandmother's Choice

57 Ladders

60 McKinley Moods

64 Millennium

68 Nine Patch Strippy

71 Progressions

75 Quartered Log Cabin

78 String Cross

81 Waterfalls

84 Finishing Your Quilt

90 Making Pillowcases and Shams

93 About the Quiltmakers

96 About the Author

Introduction

With the acceptance and ready availability of quality machine quilting, more and more quilters are making quilts for beds. Meanwhile, more people are buying queen- and king-size beds—the queen is now standard in a majority of homes—and those beds are getting thicker and thicker!

While most queen-size mattresses still measure 60" x 80" across the top, the depth of the mattresses and the box springs can vary from 9" to 12" *apiece,* and those cushy pillow tops can add as much as 6" to the total. These monstrously comfortable beds can require quilts or coverlets with drops of as much as 20" on at least three sides. Allowing for the 2" to 5" of "take-up" that can occur with heavy quilting and/or when a quilt is washed, quilters who make quilts for beds nowadays are making really big quilts!

Thus, this book. While the patterns that follow produce really big quilts—some of them will fit king-size beds—all of them are easy to make. Many of the projects are triangle free. The designs range from the classic to the contemporary, from soft and romantic to bright and bold. I'm sure you'll find more than one project you just can't wait to make!

Larger? Smaller?

If you want to make quilts larger or smaller than the sizes given, in order to fit a particular bed, try one of these strategies:

- Add or subtract a row of blocks
- Make the sashing wider or narrower
- Make the border wider or narrower
- Add or remove one or more borders

A good way to measure a large bed is to drape a 3- or 4-yard piece of fabric over the width of the mattress; fold the edges under until the drop is an appropriate length (if you're using a dust ruffle, you'll want your quilt to cover the top 2" to 4" of the ruffle). Pin at the folds, then measure the fabric from fold to fold. Repeat for the length of the mattress.

Accessories

I plan my bed quilts without pillow tucks—the top of each quilt just reaches the headboard—and complete the look with coordinating pillowcases or shams. To make accessories to go with your quilt, see "Making Pillowcases and Shams" on page 90.

Before You Begin

Read the complete cutting and piecing instructions for the quilt you plan to make before you begin. You may want to make a sample block to test the pattern and confirm your fabric choices before you proceed. Basic cutting and stitching instructions start on page 11; you'll find the information you need to finish your quilt starting on page 84.

Happy quilting, and pleasant dreams!
Judy

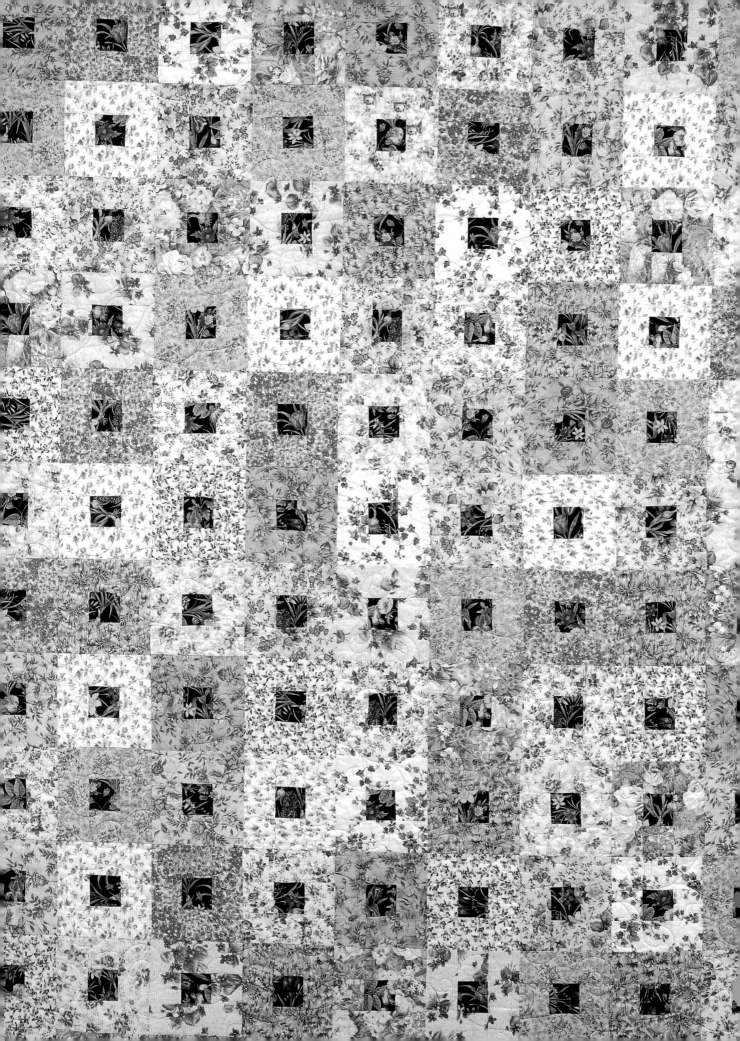

Basic Quiltmaking Instructions

This section contains general rotary-cutting, piecing, and pressing information. Tips for stitching those sometimes-tricky square-in-a-square and flying-geese units are included. Basic instructions for finishing your quilt begin on page 84.

Rotary Cutting

The quilts in this book are all rotary cut. You'll be cutting strips from fabric and cutting squares, rectangles, and triangles from some of those strips. Other strips may be joined to make strip units, which are then cut into segments.

All cutting measurements given in the pattern instructions include ¼"-wide seam allowances; don't add seam allowances to the dimensions given.

The first step in most rotary-cutting operations is to straighten the raw edge of the fabric. Fold the fabric in half lengthwise, aligning the selvages. Lay the fabric on the cutting mat with the fold of the fabric closest to you and the bulk of the fabric to your left (reverse the layout if you're left-handed).

Align a horizontal line of a long cutting ruler with the fold of the fabric. Cut along the edge of the ruler, through both layers of fabric.

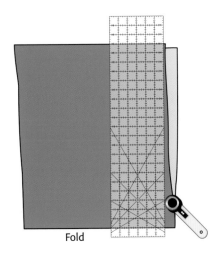

Fold

Close the safety guard on the rotary cutter immediately after making the cut. Make sure you've cut through all the fabric layers before you lift the ruler.

Move to the opposite side of the table, or rotate the cutting mat so the bulk of the fabric is to your right. If necessary, accordion-fold the fabric and pile it on the mat, being careful not to disturb your freshly cut edge.

Cut strips to the width given in the pattern instructions, measuring from the straight cut on the left. If you need a 3"-wide strip, for example, place the 3" line of the ruler on the straightened edge of the fabric. Combine a cutting square with the long ruler to make cuts wider than the long ruler allows.

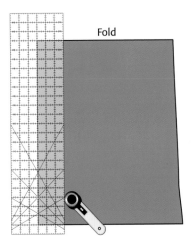

Fold

Open and check the strips occasionally to make sure your cuts are straight. If the strips develop a "bend" in the middle (a fairly common occurrence), restraighten the edge of the fabric before you proceed.

To cut squares and rectangles from a strip, straighten the selvage ends of the folded strip by aligning a horizontal line of a cutting square with the long edge of the folded strip. Cut along the edge of the ruler through both layers, removing the selvages in the process. Rotate the mat so the clean-cut end of the strip is on the left. Align the proper measurement on your cutting square with the straightened end of the strip, and cut the fabric into squares or rectangles the width of the strip. Sometimes you can get an additional piece by unfolding the strip when you reach the right-hand edge.

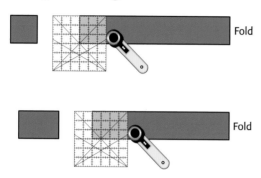

To make half-square triangles, cut squares once diagonally. To make quarter-square triangles, cut squares twice diagonally, as shown.

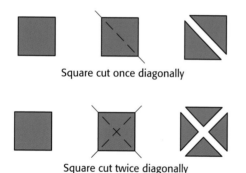

Square cut once diagonally

Square cut twice diagonally

Cutting all the way to the end of a strip (or strip unit) without counting the number of pieces cut may give you more pieces than you need to make a particular block or quilt. Use any leftovers as part of a pieced back, or toss them into the scrap bag for a future quilt.

Making and Cutting Strip Units

For many of the quilts in this book, you'll be making blocks and units by cutting strips of fabric, sewing the strips together in a particular order to make strip units, and then cutting the strip units into segments.

Make the strip units and press the seams as described in the pattern. Press from the right side first, then turn the units over and press from the wrong side to be sure that all the seam allowances face the proper direction. Press carefully to avoid stretching.

Straighten the right end of each strip unit by aligning a horizontal line of a cutting square with one of the strip unit's internal seams and cutting along the edge of the ruler. Place the straightened end on the left, align the desired measurement on your cutting square with the straightened end, and cut the required number of segments. If necessary, restraighten the end after you've made several cuts.

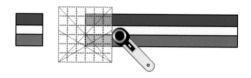

Machine Piecing and Pressing

The most important skill for a quilter to master is sewing accurate ¼" seams. If your seam allowance is off by even a few threads, your seams may not line up and your units and blocks may not be the desired finished size; this, in turn, will affect the measurements for everything else in the quilt.

Test your seam width by cutting three short strips of fabric, each exactly 2" wide. Join the pieces into a strip unit, press the seams, and measure the finished width of the center strip. If you're sewing an accurate ¼" seam, the center strip will measure exactly 1½". If it doesn't, you need to adjust or compensate for whatever you're using as a seam guide, whether it's a special ¼" sewing-machine foot, a particular needle-position setting, an engraved line on your sewing machine, or simply a piece of tape you've put on your sewing-machine bed. Some quilters find they need to sew a scant ¼"—just a thread or two short of a full ¼"—to allow for take-up when seams are pressed.

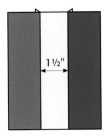

Join 2" strips and measure the center.

Press every seam before attaching a new piece of fabric. The small arrows in the construction diagrams indicate the direction in which to press the seams. When there are no arrows, press the seams however you wish.

Use plenty of heat and/or steam. Press with an up-and-down motion; moving the iron back and forth or from side to side will distort the fabric.

Snip or pull out loose threads that have been caught in the seams as you press; it's easier to tidy up the pieces when you're pressing the seams than to go back over the entire quilt later.

When sewing two pieces or units together, you may need to ease excess fabric. One piece may be slightly longer than the other due to cutting discrepancies or seam-width variations, or simply because one fabric behaves differently than another. To ease, pin the pieces together at the seams and ends—and in between, if necessary—to distribute the excess fabric. When you stitch the seam, place the shorter piece on top. The feed dogs will help ease the fullness of the longer piece.

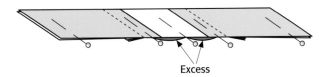

Excess

Save time and thread by chain piecing. Place the pieces that are to be joined right sides together with raw edges even; pin only where necessary. Feed the units under the presser foot one after the other without lifting the presser foot or clipping the connecting threads; backstitching isn't necessary. Clip the threads between the pieces either before or after pressing.

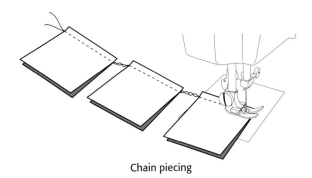

Chain piecing

It's wise to sew a complete block together before you start working in this assembly-line fashion, to ensure that the pieces have been accurately cut and to identify any piecing quirks you may need to watch out for.

Stitching Tips for Square-in-a-Square Units

Join the opposing triangles first, centering the triangles on the square. The triangle points will be sticking out about ⅜" beyond the edges of the square. Press the seams toward the triangles.

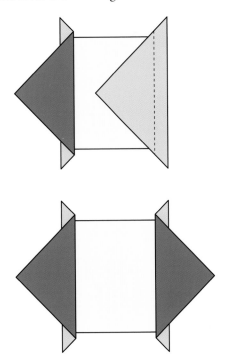

Join the remaining triangles to the square. Your ¼" seam should exactly intersect the 90° angle where the two triangles meet at both the top and bottom ends of the seam, as in the magnified areas of the drawing.

Adjust the position of the loose triangle until the seam lines up correctly at A. Take a few stitches. Then adjust the point at B and finish stitching the seam. Press the seams toward the triangles.

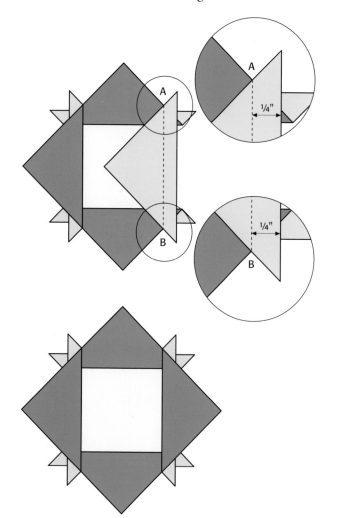

Stitching Tips for Flying-Geese Units

Join the left-hand triangle to the base triangle: Match points (A) and bottom edges; sew in the direction of the arrow. Press the seam toward the smaller triangle.

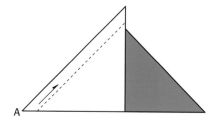

Join the right-hand triangle: Start at the arrow. Your ¼" seam should exactly intersect the 90° angle where the two smaller triangles meet, as in the magnified area of the drawing. Adjust the position of the loose triangle until the seam lines up correctly. Take a few stitches, then match points (B) and finish stitching the seam. Press the seam toward the smaller triangle.

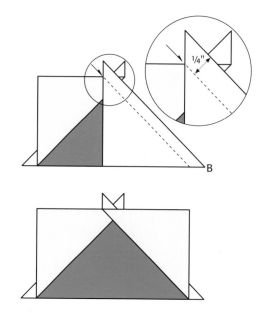

Around the Block

Pieced by Judy Dafoe Hopkins. Quilted by Mona Norris.

Finished quilt size: 96¾" x 96¾"

Finished block size: 8¾" x 8¾"

Materials

Yardages are based on 42"-wide fabrics.

4¾ yards of dark red print for alternate blocks, border, and binding

2⅛ yards of bright red print for alternate blocks

1 fat quarter (18" x 21" piece) *each* of 11 assorted tan or gold prints for blocks

9" x 16" piece *each* of 11 assorted caramel or brown prints for nine-patch units*

9" x 16" piece *each* of 11 assorted cream prints for nine-patch units*

9½ yards of fabric for backing

103" x 103" piece of batting

Use the same fabric more than once, if you wish.

Cutting

All measurements include ¼"-wide seam allowances.

From *each* of the 11 assorted cream prints, cut:

- 3 strips, 2¼" x 16" (33 total)

From *each* of the 11 assorted caramel or brown prints, cut:

- 3 strips, 2¼" x 16" (33 total)

From *each* of the 11 assorted tan or gold prints, cut:

- 2 strips, 2¼" x 21" (22 total)*

- 2 strips, 5¾" x 21" (22 total)*. From 1 strip of *each* fabric, cut 8 rectangles, 2¼" x 5¾" (88 total). Leave the remaining strips uncut.

Because the size of fat quarters can vary, the strip length (21") is approximate. Cut the strips the full length of the longest side of the fat quarter.

From the dark red print, cut:

- 1 selvage-to-selvage strip, 30" wide; set aside for alternate blocks

From the remaining dark red print, cut:

- 11 selvage-to-selvage strips, 2½" wide, for binding

From the remaining dark red print, cut:

- 4 *lengthwise* strips, 9½" x about 100", for border

Note: *For ease in construction, the quilt instructions will produce the same number of nine-patch units with light corners as with dark corners by using just two fabrics in each nine-patch unit. Some of the nine-patch units in my quilt actually use three fabrics, and I made and used more with dark corners than what is called for in the instructions.*

Making the Blocks

1. Join three 2¼" cream strips (all the same fabric) and three 2¼" caramel or brown strips (all the same fabric) to make one strip unit A and one strip unit B as shown. Press the seams toward the darker strips. Cut six segments, 2¼" wide, from each strip unit.

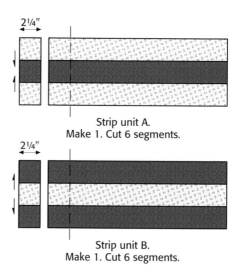

Strip unit A.
Make 1. Cut 6 segments.

Strip unit B.
Make 1. Cut 6 segments.

2. Join the step 1 segments to make two nine-patch A units and two nine-patch B units as shown. Press however you wish.

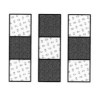

Nine-patch A unit.
Make 2.

Nine-patch B unit.
Make 2.

3. Join two matching 2¼" tan or gold strips and one 5¾" tan or gold strip of a different fabric to make one strip unit as shown. Press the seams toward the 5¾" strip. From this strip unit, cut eight segments, 2¼" wide.

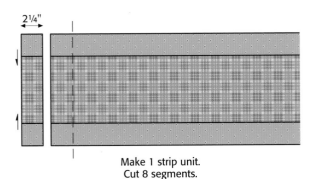

Make 1 strip unit.
Cut 8 segments.

4. Join the step 3 segments and 2¼" x 5¾" tan or gold rectangles that match the 5¾" strip you used in step 3 to the nine-patch units to make two of block A and two of block B as shown. Press the seams toward the tan or gold prints.

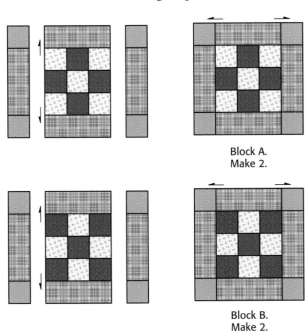

Block A.
Make 2.

Block B.
Make 2.

5. Repeat steps 1–4 with the remaining strips and rectangles to make a total of 22 of block A and 22 of block B. Because of the way the pieces are cut you will have three extra blocks, which allows flexibility when selecting blocks for the final layout.

Cutting the Alternate Blocks and Assembling the Quilt Top

1. Measure the pieced blocks through the centers to determine the size to cut the alternate blocks. If your pieced blocks were stitched perfectly, they should measure 9¼" square (raw edge to raw edge). However, they might be a little larger or smaller. If the pieced blocks measure several different sizes, determine the average measurement of the blocks.

2. From the bright red print, cut seven selvage-to-selvage strips the width determined in step 1. From these strips, cut 28 squares to the proper size (9¼" x 9¼" if your blocks came out just right).

3. From the dark red print 30" strip, cut three selvage-to-selvage strips the width determined in step 1. From these strips, cut 12 squares to the proper size (9¼" x 9¼" if your blocks came out just right).

4. Join 41 pieced blocks and the 40 dark red and bright red alternate blocks as shown to make nine horizontal rows. Place the pieced blocks randomly but pay particular attention to the placement of the dark red alternate blocks. Press the seams toward the alternate blocks.

5. Join the rows. Press the seams however you wish.

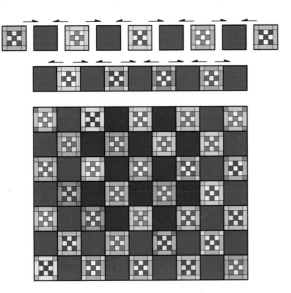

Adding the Border

1. Measure the length of the quilt through the center, from raw edge to raw edge. Cut two 9½" dark red border strips to the length measured and join them to the sides of the quilt, matching the ends and centers and easing the edges to fit. Press the seams toward the border.

2. Measure the width of the quilt through the center, including the border pieces you just added. Cut the remaining 9½" border strips to that measurement and join them to the top and bottom of the quilt as above. Press the seams toward the border.

Finishing the Quilt

For detailed instructions on finishing techniques, see "Finishing Your Quilt" on page 84.

1. Divide the backing fabric crosswise into three equal panels. Remove the selvages and join the panels with a ½" seam to make a single, large backing piece. Press the seams open.

2. Layer the quilt top with batting and backing. Baste the layers together.

3. Hand or machine quilt as desired.

4. Prepare and sew the 2½"-wide binding strips to the quilt.

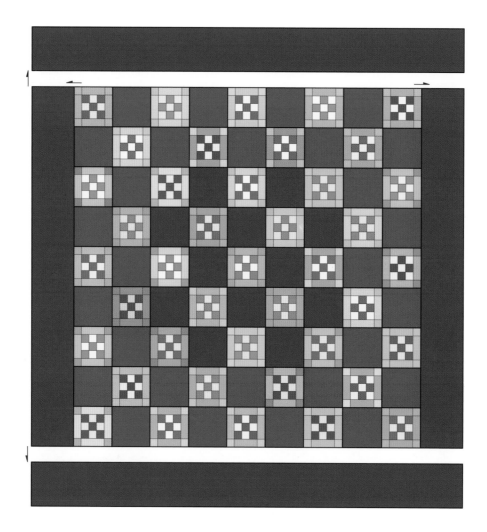

Pieced and quilted by Kathy Mosher.

Finished quilt size: 97¾" x 98"

Materials

For this quilt, choose the backing first, and then select compatible fabrics for the bars. Yardages for the red and black prints are based on 42"-wide fabrics.

A printed king-size flat sheet, at least 104" x 104", or 3 yards of 108"-wide fabric, for backing*

6 yards of red floral print for bars and binding

6 yards of black print for bars

104" x 104" piece of batting

*If you use a sheet, experienced machine quilters suggest you purchase an inexpensive sheet and wash it multiple times before the quilt is layered. Sheets with a high thread count can be difficult to machine quilt, and nearly impossible to hand quilt.

Cutting

All measurements include ¼"-wide seam allowances.

Red floral print:

Divide the red floral print crosswise into 2 equal panels.

- From the *length* of 1 of these panels, cut 6 strips, 6¼" x 98"

- From the *length* of the remaining panel, cut:

  3 strips, 6¼" x 98", for bars

  4 strips, 2½" x the length of the fabric, for binding

Black print:

Divide the black print crosswise into 2 equal panels.

- From the *length* of 1 of these panels, cut 6 strips, 6¼" x 98"

- From the *length* of the remaining panel, cut 2 strips, 6¼" x 98"

Using Leftover Fabric

Use any leftover fabric to make or trim throw pillows, pillowcases, or pillow shams. (See "Making Pillowcases and Shams" on page 90.)

Assembling the Quilt Top

Join the red and black strips as shown, matching the ends and centers and easing the edges to fit. Press the seams toward the black fabric.

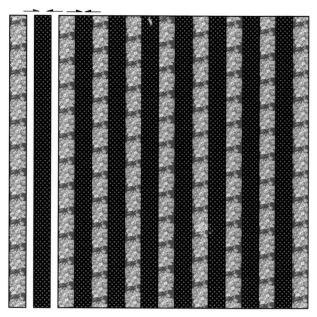

Match the ends and the centers and ease the edges to fit.

Finishing the Quilt

For detailed instructions on finishing techniques, see "Finishing Your Quilt" on page 84.

1. Layer the quilt top with batting and backing. Baste the layers together.

2. Hand or machine quilt as desired. If you used a sheet for the backing, machine quilting is the best option.

3. Prepare and sew the 2½"-wide binding strips to the quilt.

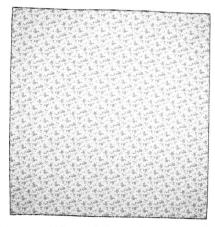

This reversible quilt has a "summer side" too!

Pieced and quilted by Kathy White.

Finished quilt size: 96½" x 99"

Materials

Yardages are based on 42"-wide fabrics. You'll need anywhere from ⅓ yard to 1 yard of 13 assorted bluish green and blue prints for the horizontal strips as specified below. These fabrics should form a value gradation that runs from light aqua to dark blue, with fabric A being the lightest and fabric M being the darkest. Tape a snip of each of these fabrics to an index card and letter the snips for reference during the cutting and sewing process.

2⅛ yards of multicolored print for vertical bars and binding

⅓ yard *each* of fabrics A and M for horizontal strips

⅝ yard *each* of fabrics B and L for horizontal strips

1 yard *each* of fabrics C through K for horizontal strips

9⅝ yards of fabric for backing. Or, combine fabric left over from making the front of the quilt with other fabrics from your stash to make a pieced backing that's at least 103" x 105".

103" x 105" piece of batting

Cutting

All measurements include ¼"-wide seam allowances.

From the multicolored print, cut:

• 8 selvage-to-selvage strips, 5" wide. From these strips, cut 143 rectangles, 2" x 5".

• 11 selvage-to-selvage strips, 2½" wide, for binding

From *each* of fabrics A and M, cut:

• 5 selvage-to-selvage strips, 2" wide (10 total)

From *each* of fabrics B and L, cut:

• 10 selvage-to-selvage strips, 2" wide (20 total)

From *each* of fabrics C through K, cut:

• 15 selvage-to-selvage strips, 2" wide (135 total)

Making the Rows

1. Join the 2" strips of fabrics A, B, and C as shown to make five strip units. The lightest of the three fabrics should be at the top of the strip units, and the darkest at the bottom. Press the seams however you wish. From *four* of the strip units, cut a total of 12 segments, 13" wide. From the fifth strip unit, cut one segment, 13" wide, and two segments, 6" wide.

From 4 of the strip units, cut 12 segments, 13" wide.

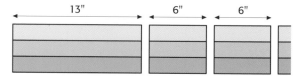

From the fifth strip unit, cut 1 segment, 13" wide, and 2 segments, 6" wide.

2. Join the segments you cut in step 1 and 13 of the 2" x 5" multicolored print rectangles to make rows 1 and 2. Use seven 13" strip-unit segments and six multicolored rectangles for row 1. Use six 13" strip-unit segments, two 6" strip-unit segments, and seven multicolored rectangles for row 2. Press the seams however you wish.

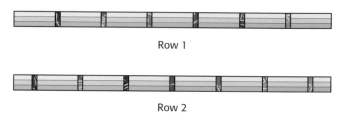

Row 1

Row 2

3. Repeat steps 1 and 2 using fabrics B, C, and D to make rows 3 and 4.

4. Repeat steps 1 and 2 using fabrics C, D, and E to make rows 5 and 6.

5. Repeat steps 1 and 2 using fabrics D, E, and F to make rows 7 and 8.

6. Repeat steps 1 and 2 using fabrics E, F, and G to make rows 9 and 10.

7. Repeat steps 1 and 2 using fabrics F, G, and H to make rows 11 and 12.

8. Repeat steps 1 and 2 using fabrics G, H, and I to make rows 13 and 14.

9. Repeat steps 1 and 2 using fabrics H, I, and J to make rows 15 and 16.

10. Repeat steps 1 and 2 using fabrics I, J, and K to make rows 17 and 18.

11. Repeat steps 1 and 2 using fabrics J, K, and L to make rows 19 and 20.

12. Repeat steps 1 and 2 using fabrics K, L, and M to make rows 21 and 22.

Assembling the Quilt Top

Join the rows as shown, aligning the multicolored print rectangles in the even rows and the multicolored print rectangles in the odd rows. Press the seams however you wish.

Finishing the Quilt

For detailed instructions on finishing techniques, see "Finishing Your Quilt" on page 84.

1. Divide the backing fabric crosswise into three equal panels. Remove the selvages and join the panels with a ½" seam to make a single, large backing piece. Press the seams open.

2. Layer the quilt top with batting and backing. Baste the layers together.

3. Hand or machine quilt as desired.

4. Prepare and sew the 2½"-wide binding strips to the quilt.

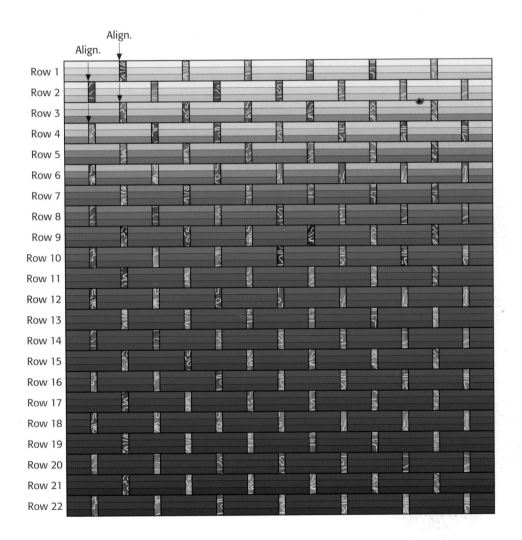

Blocks in a Box

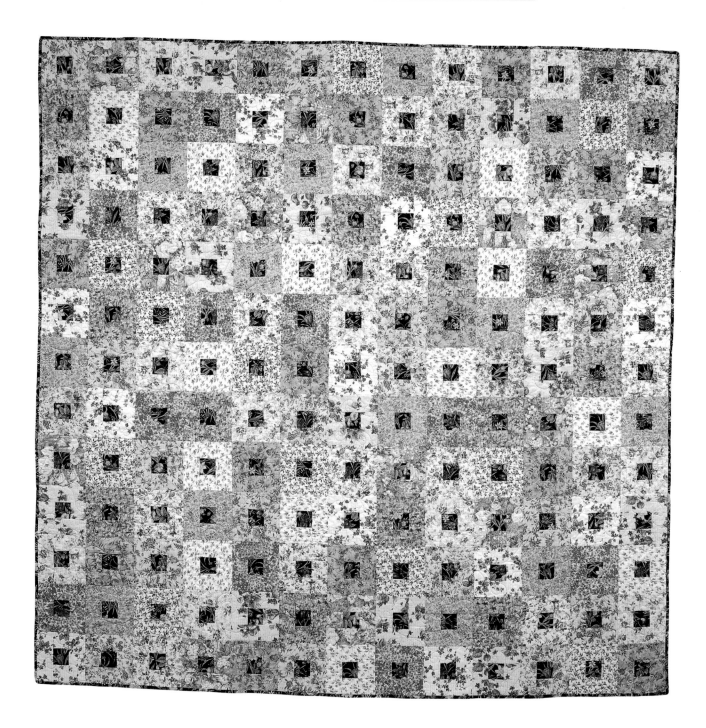

Pieced by Clare Brooks. Quilted by Tracey Dukowitz.

Finished quilt size: **97½" x 97½"**
Finished block size: **7½" x 7½"**

Materials

Yardages are based on 42"-wide fabrics.

2⅛ yards of black floral print for block centers and binding

¾ yard *each* of 13 assorted light floral prints for blocks

9⅝ yards of fabric for backing. Or, combine fabric left over from making the front of the quilt with other fabrics from your stash to make a pieced backing that's at least 104" x 104".

104" x 104" piece of batting

Cutting

All measurements include ¼"-wide seam allowances.

From *each* of the 13 assorted light floral prints, cut:

- 2 selvage-to-selvage strips, 8" wide (26 total). From *each* of these strips, cut 13 rectangles, 3" x 8" (338 total).
- 2 selvage-to-selvage strips, 3" wide (26 total)

From the black floral print, cut:

- 13 selvage-to-selvage strips, 3" wide
- 11 selvage-to-selvage strips, 2½" wide, for binding

Making the Blocks

1. Join two matching 3" light print strips to a 3" black print strip to make one strip unit. Press the seams toward the black print. From this strip unit, cut 13 segments, 3" wide.

Make 1 strip unit.
Cut 13 segments.

2. Join matching 3" x 8" light print rectangles to the segments you cut in step 1 to make 13 blocks. Press the seams however you wish.

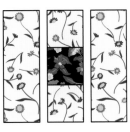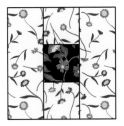

Make 13.

3. Repeats steps 1 and 2 with the remaining 3" light and black print strips and 3" x 8" light print rectangles to make a total of 169 blocks, 13 in each fabric combination.

Assembling the Quilt Top

1. Join the blocks to make seven of row 1 and six of row 2, each containing 13 blocks. *Rotate every other block as shown.* Press the seams toward the blocks with the vertical seams.

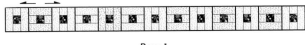

Row 1.
Make 7.

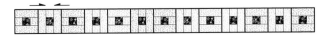

Row 2.
Make 6.

2. Join the rows as shown in the photo on page 24. Press the seams however you wish.

Finishing the Quilt

For detailed instructions on finishing techniques, see "Finishing Your Quilt" on page 84.

1. Divide the backing fabric crosswise into three equal panels. Remove the selvages and join the panels with a ½" seam to make a single, large backing piece. Press the seams open.

2. Layer the quilt top with batting and backing. Baste the layers together.

3. Hand or machine quilt as desired.

4. Prepare and sew the 2½"-wide binding strips to the quilt.

Burgoyne Surrounded

Pieced and quilted by Carol Parks.

Finished quilt size: 95" x 95"
Finished block size: 15" x 15"

Materials

Yardages are based on 42"-wide fabrics.

9¾ yards of tan print for background, sashing, borders, and binding

2¼ yards of brown print for blocks and checked border

9¼ yards of fabric for backing

101" x 101" piece of batting

Cutting

All measurements include ¼"-wide seam allowances.

From the tan print, cut:

- A 2-yard piece; set aside for sashing

From the remaining piece of tan print, cut:

- 39 selvage-to-selvage strips, 1½" wide

- 12 selvage-to-selvage strips, 2½" wide (10 are for binding)

- 6 selvage-to-selvage strips, 5½" wide. From these strips, cut 64 rectangles, 3½" x 5½".

- 8 selvage-to-selvage strips, 3½" wide. From these strips, cut 128 rectangles, 2½" x 3½".

From the *length* of the remaining piece of tan print, cut:

- 4 strips, 7½" wide x at least 98" long, for outer border

- 4 strips, 2½" wide x at least 82" long, for inner border

From scraps of the tan print, cut:

- 1 square, 1½" x 1½"

From the brown print, cut:

- 41 selvage-to-selvage strips, 1½" wide

- 4 selvage-to-selvage strips, 2½" wide

- 1 square, 1½" x 1½"

Making the Blocks

1. Join 2½" tan strips, a 1½" brown strip, 2½" brown strips, and 1½" tan strips to make one of strip unit A and two of strip unit B as shown. Press the seams toward the brown strips. From these strip units, cut the number of 1½"-wide and 2½"-wide segments indicated.

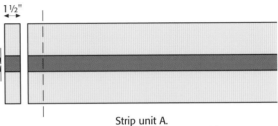

Strip unit A.
Make 1. Cut 16 segments, 1½" wide.

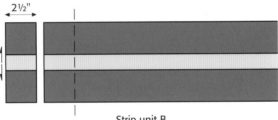

Strip unit B.
Make 2. Cut 32 segments, 2½" wide.

2. Join the segments you cut in step 1 to make 16 center units as shown. Press the seams however you wish.

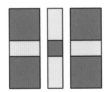

Center unit.
Make 16.

3. Join 1½" tan strips and 1½" brown strips to make seven of strip unit C and four of strip unit D as shown. Press the seams toward the brown strips. From these strip units, cut the number of 1½"-wide segments indicated.

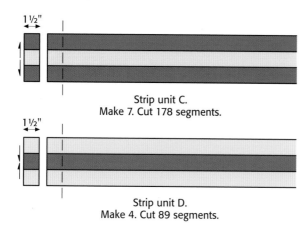

Strip unit C.
Make 7. Cut 178 segments.

Strip unit D.
Make 4. Cut 89 segments.

4. Join the segments you cut in step 3 to make 89 nine-patch units as shown. Press the seams however you wish.

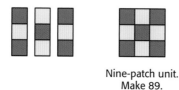

Nine-patch unit.
Make 89.

5. Join the remaining 1½" tan and brown strips to make 22 of strip unit E as shown. Press the seams toward the dark strips. From 8 of these strip units, cut 128 segments, 2½" wide. From the 14 remaining strip units, cut 348 segments, 1½" wide. Set 156 of these segments aside to use for the checked border.

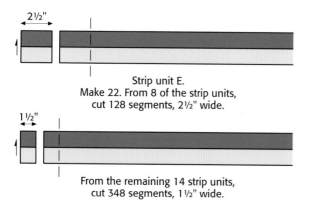

Strip unit E.
Make 22. From 8 of the strip units,
cut 128 segments, 2½" wide.

From the remaining 14 strip units,
cut 348 segments, 1½" wide.

6. Join the 2½" segments and 64 of the 1½" segments from step 5 to make 64 pieced rectangle units as shown. Join 128 of the remaining 1½" segments to make 64 four-patch units as shown. Press the seams however you wish.

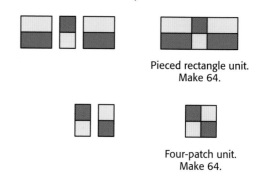

Pieced rectangle unit.
Make 64.

Four-patch unit.
Make 64.

7. Join the pieced rectangle units from step 6 and the 3½" x 5½" tan rectangles to make 64 side units as shown. Press the seams toward the rectangles.

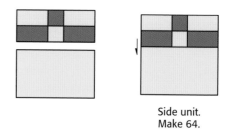

Side unit.
Make 64.

8. Join 64 nine-patch units, 64 four-patch units, and the 2½" x 3½" tan rectangles to make 64 corner units as shown. Press the seams toward the rectangles.

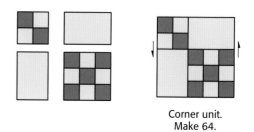

Corner unit.
Make 64.

9. Join the center, side, and corner units to make 16 Burgoyne Surrounded blocks as shown. Press the seams as indicated.

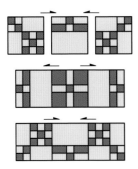
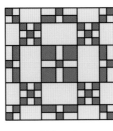
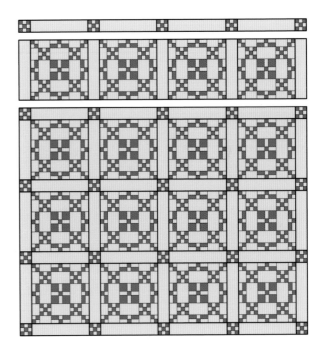

Make 16.

Cutting the Sashing

1. Measure the Burgoyne Surrounded blocks and the remaining nine-patch units through the centers to determine the size to cut the sashing strips. If your blocks were stitched perfectly, the Burgoyne Surrounded blocks should measure 15½" square (raw edge to raw edge) and the nine-patch units should measure 3½" square (raw edge to raw edge). However, they might be a little larger or smaller. If the blocks measure several different sizes, determine the average measurement of the Burgoyne Surrounded blocks and the average measurement of the nine-patch units.

2. From the 2-yard piece of tan fabric you set aside previously, cut four selvage-to-selvage strips the width determined in step 1 for the *Burgoyne Surrounded* blocks.

3. From the strips you cut in step 2, cut 40 segments the width determined in step 1 for the *nine-patch* units.

Assembling the Quilt Top

1. Join the nine-patch units and sashing pieces to make five sashing rows and four block rows as shown. If you used average measurements, you can take care of any minor discrepancies by easing either the blocks or the sashing pieces as you sew. Press the seams toward the sashing pieces.

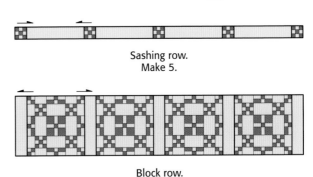

Sashing row.
Make 5.

Block row.
Make 4.

2. Join the rows as shown. Press the seams however you wish.

Adding the Borders

1. Measure the length of the quilt through the center, from raw edge to raw edge. Cut two 2½" tan border strips to the length measured and join them to the sides of the quilt, matching the ends and centers and easing the edges to fit. Press the seams toward the border.

2. Measure the width of the quilt through the center, including the border pieces you just added. Cut the remaining 2½" tan border strips to that measurement and join them to the top and bottom of the quilt as above. Press the seams toward the border.

3. Join the remaining 1½" strip-unit segments and the loose 1½" tan and brown squares to make checked border strips as shown. Use 38 strip-unit segments and the brown square for the left border and 38 strip-unit segments and the tan square for the right border. Use 40 strip-unit segments each for the top and bottom strips. Join the side strips first, and then the top and bottom strips, matching the ends and centers and easing the edges to fit.

4. Repeat steps 1 and 2 with the 7½" tan strips for the outer border.

Finishing the Quilt

For detailed instructions on finishing techniques, see "Finishing Your Quilt" on page 84.

1. Divide the backing fabric crosswise into three equal panels. Remove the selvages and join the panels with a ½" seam to make a single, large backing piece. Press the seams open.

2. Layer the quilt top with batting and backing. Baste the layers together.

3. Hand or machine quilt as desired.

4. Prepare and sew the 2½"-wide binding strips to the quilt.

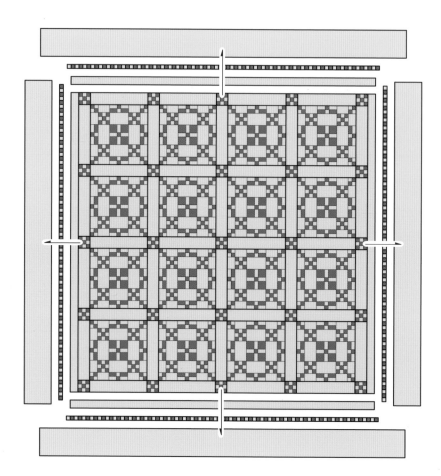

Cornucopia

Pieced by Janet Strait Gorton. Quilted by Kathy Mosher.

Finished quilt size: 102½" x 102½"

Finished block size: 10¼" x 10¼"

Materials

Yardages are based on 42"-wide fabrics.

6¼ yards of white-on-white print for blocks and binding

1 strip *exactly* 6" wide and at least 39" long *each* of 34 assorted Asian prints for blocks*

9⅞ yards of fabric for backing

108" x 108" piece of batting

Use the same fabric more than once, if you wish.

Cutting

All measurements include ¼ "-wide seam allowances.

From *each* of the 34 Asian-print strips, cut:

• 6 squares, 6" x 6" (204 total). Cut 200 of these squares once diagonally to make 400 half-square triangles. Set the remaining 4 squares aside for another project.

From the white-on-white print, cut:

• 18 selvage-to-selvage strips, 7¾" wide. From these strips, cut 86 squares, 7¾" x 7¾", cutting just 1 square from the 18th strip.

• 3 selvage-to-selvage strips, 11½" wide. From these strips, cut 7 squares, 11½" x 11½", cutting just 1 square from the 3rd strip. Cut the squares twice diagonally to make 28 quarter-square triangles. You will use 26 and have 2 left over.

• 11 selvage-to-selvage strips, 2½" wide, for binding

From scraps of the white-on-white print, cut:

• 2 squares, 6" x 6". Cut the squares once diagonally to make 4 half-square triangles.

Making the Blocks

1. Join 6" Asian print half-square triangles and the 7¾" white-on-white squares to make 86 square-in-a-square units. (See "Stitching Tips for Square-in-a-Square Units" on page 13.) Use a different Asian print in each corner. Press the seams toward the Asian prints.

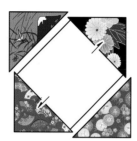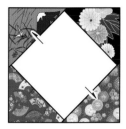

Square-in-a-square unit.
Make 86.

2. Join 6" Asian print half-square triangles and the 11½" white-on-white quarter-square triangles to make 26 flying-geese units. (See "Stitching Tips for Flying-Geese Units" on page 14.) Use a different Asian print in each corner. Press the seams toward the Asian prints.

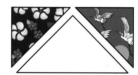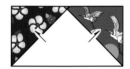

Flying-geese unit.
Make 26.

3. Join the remaining 6" Asian print half-square triangles and the 6" white-on-white half-square triangles to make four half-square-triangle units. Press the seams toward the Asian prints.

Half-square-
triangle unit.
Make 4.

Assembling the Quilt Top

1. Join the units you made in the previous steps to make two of row A, five of row B, and four of row C.

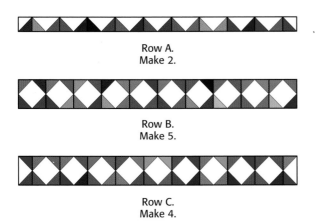

Row A.
Make 2.

Row B.
Make 5.

Row C.
Make 4.

2. Join the rows, reversing the bottom row A to complete the pattern as shown. Press the seams however you wish.

Finishing the Quilt

For detailed instructions on finishing techniques, see "Finishing Your Quilt" on page 84.

1. Divide the backing fabric crosswise into three equal panels. Remove the selvages and join the panels with a ½" seam to make a single, large backing piece. Press the seams open.

2. Layer the quilt top with batting and backing. Baste the layers together.

3. Hand or machine quilt as desired.

4. Prepare and sew the 2½"-wide binding strips to the quilt.

Checkers

Pieced by Sarah Kaufman. Quilted by Deanna Smith.

Finished quilt size: 97" x 97"

Materials

Yardages are based on 42"-wide fabrics.

6⅞ yards of dark rust print for sashing, border, and binding

1⅝ yards of rust solid for squares

1⅛ yards of taupe print for sashing squares

1⅛ yards of geometric rust print for squares

⅔ yard of swirly rust print for squares

9½ yards of fabric for backing. Or, combine fabric left over from making the front of the quilt with other fabrics from your stash to make a pieced backing that's at least 103" x 103".

103" x 103" piece of batting

Cutting

All measurements include ¼"-wide seam allowances.

From the dark rust print, cut:

- 12 selvage-to-selvage strips, 5½" wide. From 1 of these strips, cut 11 rectangles, 3" x 5½". Leave the remaining strips uncut.
- 19 selvage-to-selvage strips, 3" wide

From the *length* of the remaining piece of dark rust print, cut:

- 4 strips, 6½" wide x at least 99" long, for border
- 4 strips, 2½" wide, for binding

From the geometric rust print, cut:

- 6 selvage-to-selvage strips, 5½" wide

From the swirly rust print, cut:

- 4 selvage-to-selvage strips, 5½" wide

From the rust solid, cut:

- 9 selvage-to-selvage strips, 5½" wide

From the taupe print, cut:

- 12 selvage-to-selvage strips, 3" wide. From 1 of these strips, cut 12 squares, 3" x 3". Leave the remaining strips uncut.

Making the Units and Assembling the Quilt Top

1. Join six of the 3" dark rust strips and the 5½" geometric print strips to make six strip units as shown. Press the seams toward the dark rust strips. From these strip units, cut 36 segments, 5½" wide.

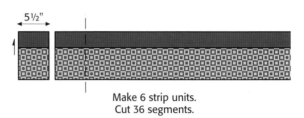

5½"

Make 6 strip units.
Cut 36 segments.

2. Join four of the 3" dark rust strips and the 5½" swirly print strips to make four strip units as shown. Press the seams toward the dark rust strips. From these strip units, cut 25 segments, 5½" wide.

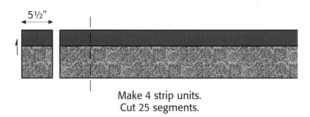

5½"

Make 4 strip units.
Cut 25 segments.

3. Join the remaining nine 3" dark rust strips and the 5½" rust solid strips to make nine strip units as shown. Press the seams toward the dark rust strips. From these strip units, cut 60 segments, 5½" wide.

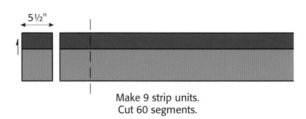

5½"

Make 9 strip units.
Cut 60 segments.

4. Join the 3" taupe print strips and the 5½" dark rust strips to make 11 strip units as shown. Press

the seams toward the dark rust strips. From these strip units, cut 132 segments, 3" wide.

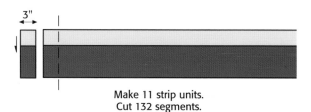

Make 11 strip units.
Cut 132 segments.

5. Join the segments you cut in step 4 and the loose 3" taupe print squares to make 12 of row 1. Press the seams toward the dark rust print.

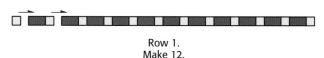

Row 1.
Make 12.

6. Join the segments you cut in steps 1–3 and the loose 3" x 5½" dark rust rectangles to make six of row 2 and five of row 3. Press the seams toward the dark rust rectangles.

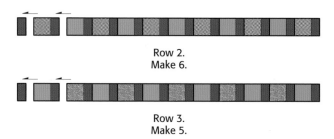

Row 2.
Make 6.

Row 3.
Make 5.

7. Join the rows as shown. Press the seams however you wish.

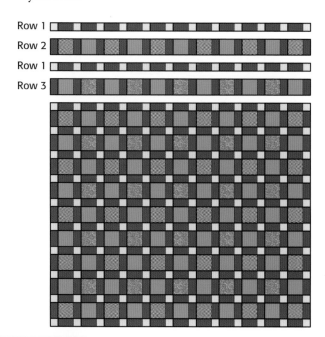

Row 1
Row 2
Row 1
Row 3

Adding the Border

1. Measure the length of the quilt through the center, from raw edge to raw edge. Cut two of the 6½" dark rust border strips to the length measured and join them to the sides of the quilt, matching the ends and centers and easing the edges to fit. Press the seams toward the border.

2. Measure the width of the quilt through the center, including the border pieces you just added. Cut the remaining two border strips to that measurement and join them to the top and bottom of the quilt as above. Press the seams toward the border.

Finishing the Quilt

For detailed instructions on finishing techniques, see "Finishing Your Quilt" on page 84.

1. Divide the backing fabric crosswise into three equal panels. Remove the selvages and join the panels with a ½" seam to make a single, large backing piece. Press the seams open.

2. Layer the quilt top with batting and backing. Baste the layers together.

3. Hand or machine quilt as desired.

4. Prepare and sew the 2½"-wide binding strips to the quilt.

Courthouse Stars

Pieced by Nellie Oldaker. Quilted by Amy D. Helmkamp and Linda Humfeld.

Finished quilt size: 98" x 98"

Finished block size: 18" x 18"

Materials

Yardages are based on 42"-wide fabrics.

6¾ yards of tan print for background and border

3⅜ yards of green print for blocks and binding

2⅝ yards of wine print for blocks

9⅝ yards of fabric for backing. Or, combine fabric left over from making the front of the quilt with other fabrics from your stash to make a pieced backing that's at least 104" x 104".

104" x 104" piece of batting

Cutting

All measurements include ¼ "-wide seam allowances.

From the wine print, cut:

• 15 selvage-to-selvage strips, 5½" wide

From the green print, cut:

• 15 selvage-to-selvage strips, 5½" wide

• 11 selvage-to-selvage strips, 2½" wide, for binding

From the tan print, cut:

• 18 selvage-to-selvage strips, 1½" wide

• 4 selvage-to-selvage strips, 3½" wide

• 4 selvage-to-selvage strips, 5½" wide

• 3 selvage-to-selvage strips, 7½" wide

• 3 selvage-to-selvage strips, 11½" wide. From these strips, cut 9 squares, 11½" x 11½".

From the *length* of the remaining tan print, cut:

• 2 strips, 11½" wide x at least 100" long. From these strips, cut 16 squares, 11½" x 11½".

• 4 strips, 4" wide x at least 100" long, for border

From scraps of the remaining tan print, cut:

• 2 squares, 1½" x 1½"

Making the Blocks

Important Note: *Always check the orientation of the wine and green segments before you sew! Press the strip-unit seams toward the darker fabric throughout. When you join the strip-unit segments to the larger units, press the seams away from the tan squares.*

1. Join 5½" wine strips, 1½" tan strips, and 5½" green strips to make two of strip unit A. From these strip units, cut 50 segments, 1½" wide.

   Join the segments to the tops and bottoms of the 11½" tan squares. Make 25.

   Note: *The wine print is on the right at the top of the squares, and on the left at the bottom of the squares.*

1½"

Strip unit A.
Make 2. Cut 50 segments.

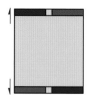

Make 25.

2. Join 1½" tan strips, 5½" wine strips, and 5½" green strips to make two of strip unit B. From these strip units, cut 50 segments, 1½" wide.

   Join the segments to the left and right sides of the tan squares as shown.

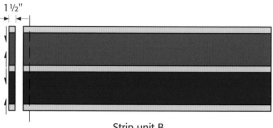

1½"

Strip unit B.
Make 2. Cut 50 segments.

3. Join 5½" wine strips, 3½" tan strips, and 5½" green strips to make two of strip unit C. From these strip units, cut 50 segments, 1½" wide.

Join the segments to the tops and bottoms of the units you made in step 2 as shown.

1½"

Strip unit C.
Make 2. Cut 50 segments.

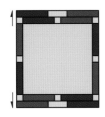

4. Join 1½" tan strips, 5½" wine strips, 3½" tan strips, and 5½" green strips to make two of strip unit D. From these strip units, cut 50 segments, 1½" wide.

Join the segments to the left and right sides of the units you made in step 3 as shown.

1½"

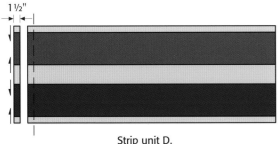

Strip unit D.
Make 2. Cut 50 segments.

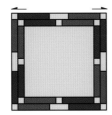

5. Join 5½" wine strips, 5½" tan strips, and 5½" green strips to make two of strip unit E. From these strip units, cut 50 segments, 1½" wide.

Join the segments to the tops and bottoms of the units you made in step 4 as shown.

1½"

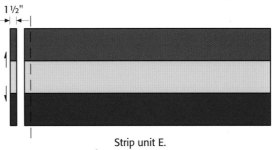

Strip unit E.
Make 2. Cut 50 segments.

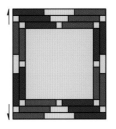

6. Join 1½" tan strips, 5½" wine strips, 5½" tan strips, and 5½" green strips to make two of strip unit F. From these strip units, cut 50 segments, 1½" wide.

Join the segments to the left and right sides of the units you made in step 5 as shown.

1½"

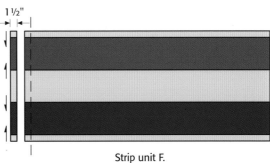

Strip unit F.
Make 2. Cut 50 segments.

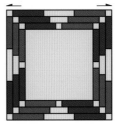

7. Join a 5½" wine strip, a 7½" tan strip, and a 5½" green strip to make one strip unit G. From this strip unit, cut 26 segments, 1½" wide.

Join 25 of these segments to the *bottom edges* of the units you made in step 6 as shown. *Set the remaining segment aside to use in step 9.*

1½"

Strip unit G.
Make 1. Cut 26 segments.

8. Join 5½" wine strips, 7½" tan strips, 5½" green strips, and 1½" tan strips to make two of strip unit H. From these strip units, cut 34 segments, 1½" wide.

Join 25 of these segments to the *right edges* of the units you made in step 7 as shown. *Set the remaining segments aside to use in step 9.*

1½"

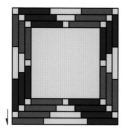

Strip unit H.
Make 2. Cut 34 segments.

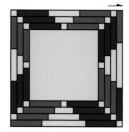

9. Join the remaining unit G and H segments and the 1½" tan squares to make sashing strips for the left side and the top of the quilt as shown. Press the seams toward the darker fabrics.

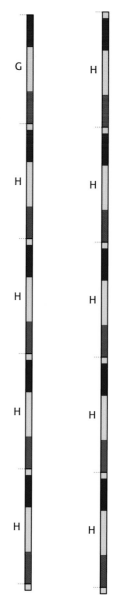

Left side sashing   Top sashing

Assembling the Quilt Top

1. Join the blocks to make five horizontal rows as shown. *Check the orientation of the wine and green prints before you sew.* Press the seams in opposite directions from row to row.

2. Join the rows. Press the seams however you wish.

3. Join the sashing strips to the left side and the top of the quilt as shown below.

Adding the Border

1. Measure the length of the quilt through the center, from raw edge to raw edge. Cut two 4"-wide tan border strips to the length measured and join them to the sides of the quilt, matching the ends and centers and easing the edges to fit. Press the seams toward the border.

2. Measure the width of the quilt through the center, including the border pieces you just added. Cut the remaining two border strips to that measurement and join them to the top and bottom of the quilt as above. Press the seams toward the border.

Finishing the Quilt

For detailed instructions on finishing techniques, see "Finishing Your Quilt" on page 84.

1. Divide the backing fabric crosswise into three equal panels. Remove the selvages and join the panels with a ½" seam to make a single, large backing piece. Press the seams open.

2. Layer the quilt top with batting and backing. Baste the layers together.

3. Hand or machine quilt as desired.

4. Prepare and sew the 2½"-wide binding strips to the quilt.

Double Nine Patch

Pieced by Judy Dafoe Hopkins. Quilted by Carol Parks.

Finished quilt size: 94¾" x 94¾"

Finished block size: 11¼" x 11¼"

Materials

Yardages are based on 42"-wide fabrics.

6 yards of white-and-blue striped print for border*

3 yards of indigo print for blocks and binding

2⅝ yards of white print for sashing

1 fat quarter (18" x 21" piece) *each* of 15 assorted white prints for blocks

9¼ yards of fabric for backing. Or, combine fabric left over from making the front of the quilt with other fabrics from your stash to make a pieced backing that's at least 101" x 101".

101" x 101" piece of batting

This yardage calculation is based on a striped print that has three usable repeats across the width of the fabric. You'll have a lot of this fabric left over after you've cut four border strips. Use it as part of a pieced backing or to make or trim pillowcases or shams. (See "Making Pillowcases and Shams" on page 90.)

If you use a plain, allover print for the border and cut lengthwise strips 9½" wide or less, 3 yards will be adequate.

Cutting

All measurements include ¼"-wide seam allowances.

From *each* of the 15 assorted white prints, cut:

- 4 strips, 1¾" x 21" (60 total)*
- 2 strips, 4¼" x 21" (30 total)*. From these strips, cut 100 squares, 4¼" x 4¼".

Because the size of fat quarters can vary, the strip length (21") is approximate. Cut the strips the full length of the longest side of the fat quarter.

From the indigo print, cut:

- 38 selvage-to-selvage strips, 1¾" wide. Cut these strips widthwise to make 76 strips, 1¾" x about 21". You will use 75 and have 1 left over.
- 11 selvage-to-selvage strips, 2½" wide, for binding

White-and-blue striped print:

Divide the white-and-blue striped print crosswise into 2 equal panels.

- From the *length* of one of these panels, cut 3 strips, about 8½" wide (depending on the design in the fabric), for border
- From the *length* of the remaining panel, cut 1 strip, about 8½" wide, for border

Making the Blocks

1. Join four 1¾" white print strips (all the same fabric) and five 1¾" indigo print strips to make one of strip unit A and two of strip unit B as shown. Press the seams toward the indigo strips. Cut the number of 1¾"-wide segments indicated from each strip unit.

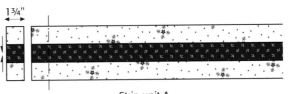

Strip unit A.
Make 1. Cut 11 segments.

Strip unit B.
Make 2. Cut 22 segments.

2. Join the segments you cut in step 1 to make 11 nine-patch units as shown. Press the seams however you wish.

Make 11.

3. Repeat steps 1 and 2 with the remaining 1¾" white and indigo print strips to make a total of 165 nine-patch units. You will have four extra, which provides more layout options.

4. Join 125 of the nine-patch units and the 4¼" white squares to make 25 Double Nine Patch

blocks. Combine the fabrics at random. Press the seams as indicated.

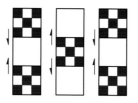

Make 25.

Cutting the Sashing

1. Measure the Double Nine Patch blocks and the remaining nine-patch units through the centers to determine the size to cut the sashing strips. If your blocks were stitched perfectly, the Double Nine Patch blocks should measure 11¾" square (raw edge to raw edge) and the nine-patch units should measure 4¼" square (raw edge to raw edge). However, they might be a little larger or smaller. If the blocks measure several different sizes, determine the average measurement of the Double Nine Patch blocks and the average measurement of the nine-patch units.

2. From the white print sashing fabric, cut seven selvage-to-selvage strips the width determined in step 1 for the *Double Nine Patch* blocks.

3. From the strips you cut in step 2, cut 60 segments the width determined in step 1 for the *nine-patch* units.

Assembling the Quilt Top

1. Join the remaining nine-patch units, the Double Nine Patch blocks, and the sashing pieces to make six sashing rows and five block rows as shown. If you used average measurements, you can take care of any minor discrepancies by easing either the blocks or the sashing pieces as you sew. Press the seams toward the sashing pieces.

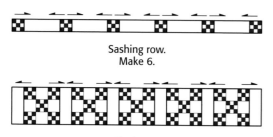

Sashing row.
Make 6.

Block row.
Make 5.

2. Join the rows as shown in the photo on page 42. Press the seams however you wish.

Adding the Border

For detailed instructions on making mitered borders, see "Borders with Mitered Corners" on page 85.

1. Measure the width and length of the quilt through the center, from raw edge to raw edge. Mark the lengthwise measurement on two of the white-and-blue border strips with pins, leaving an equal amount at each end. Pin the strips to the sides of the quilt with the raw top and bottom edges of the quilt even with the pins. Join the strips to the quilt, starting and stopping the stitching ¼" from the corners of the quilt. Press the seams toward the border.

2. Mark the widthwise measurement on the remaining two border strips with pins, leaving an equal amount at each end. Pin and stitch to the top and bottom of the quilt as in step 1.

3. Miter the corners, following the instructions on page 85.

Finishing the Quilt

For detailed instructions on finishing techniques, see "Finishing Your Quilt" on page 84.

1. Divide the backing fabric crosswise into three equal panels. Remove the selvages and join the panels with a ½" seam to make a single, large backing piece. Press the seams open.

2. Layer the quilt top with batting and backing. Baste the layers together.

3. Hand or machine quilt as desired.

4. Prepare and sew the 2½"-wide binding stips to the quilt.

Far West

Pieced by Michele A. Hall. Quilted by Michelle Gwin.

Finished quilt size: 95½" x 94½"

Finished block size: 13½" x 13½"

Materials

Yardages are based on 42"-wide fabrics. The yardage requirements call for two dark fabrics in each of four color groups. For the A fabric in each group, choose a solid or a tone-on-tone print that "reads" like a solid. The B fabric should be the same color as the A fabric, and very close in value, but different in visual texture.

3⅞ yards of light print for block backgrounds

1½ yards of cranberry A fabric, print or solid

1½ yards of purple A fabric, print or solid

1½ yards of black A fabric, print or solid

1½ yards of green A fabric, print or solid

½ yard of cranberry B print

½ yard of purple B print

½ yard of black B print

½ yard of green B print

⅞ yard of multicolored print for binding

9⅜ yards of fabric for backing. Or, combine fabric left over from making the front of the quilt with other fabrics from your stash to make a pieced backing that's at least 102" x 102".

102" x 102" piece of batting

Cutting

All measurements include ¼ "-wide seam allowances.

From *each* of the four A fabrics, cut:

- 5 selvage-to-selvage strips, 2" wide (20 total)
- 3 selvage-to-selvage strips, 5⅜" wide (12 total)
- 5 selvage-to-selvage strips, 4" wide (20 total), for seamed borders

From *each* of the four B fabrics, cut:

- 7 selvage-to-selvage strips, 2" wide (28 total)

From the light print, cut:

- 30 selvage-to-selvage strips, 2" wide
- 12 selvage-to-selvage strips, 5⅜" wide

From the multicolored print, cut:

- 10 selvage-to-selvage strips, 2½" wide, for binding

Making the Blocks

This is one of those designs that creates an occasional pressing conundrum no matter what you do. If you press the seams open, you may have difficulty matching seams, and you'll have no "ditch" to stitch in when you reach the quilting stage. If you press to the side, you may have to twist some seams on the back when you assemble the blocks and/or the quilt to make them butt together properly for easy joining. You choose.

1. Using the 5⅜" light strips and the 5⅜" A strips, make 144 half-square-triangle units (36 of each fabric combination), following the instructions below:

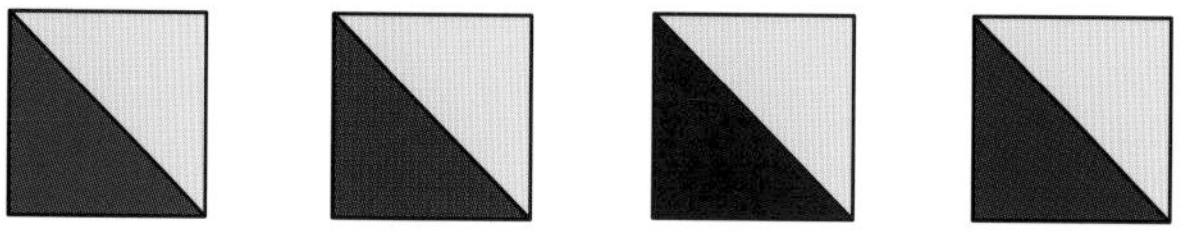

Cranberry A.   Purple A.   Black A.   Green A.
Make 36.   Make 36.   Make 36.   Make 36.

Layer the 5⅜" A strips and the 5⅜" light strips, right sides together, to make 12 contrasting strip pairs. Don't stitch these strips together! You may want to lightly press the strip pairs to make the fabrics "stick together" before you proceed.

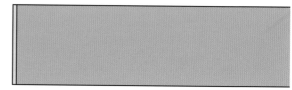

Place strips right sides together, aligning the long edges.

Cut six squares, 5⅜" x 5⅜", from each layered strip pair (72 layered pairs total).

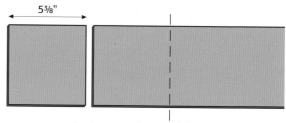

5⅜"

Cut 6 squares from each layered strip pair (72 layered pairs total).

Cut the layered squares once diagonally, from corner to corner.

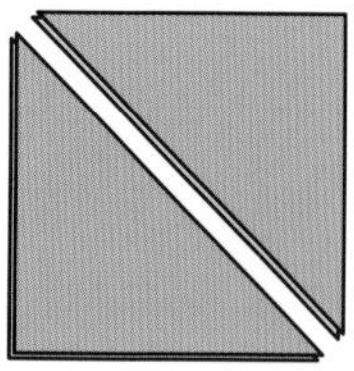

Chain stitch the resulting triangle pairs along the long edges to make half-square-triangle units; the pairs are already matched and ready to sew. Press the seams open or toward the darker triangles. You'll have one extra half-square-triangle unit in each fabric combination; set these aside for another project.

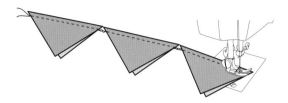

2. Join 2" light and 2" A and B strips to make strip units in four color combinations as shown. Press the seams open or toward the darker fabrics. Cut 35 segments, 5" wide, from the strip units of each color combination.

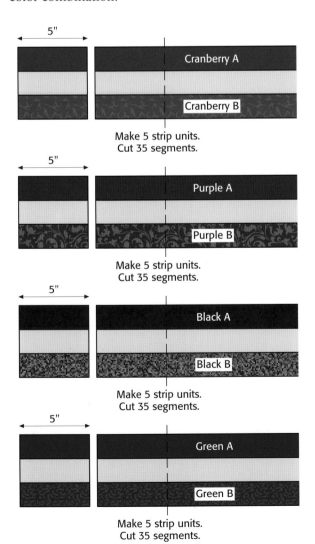

5"

Cranberry A

Cranberry B

Make 5 strip units.
Cut 35 segments.

5"

Purple A

Purple B

Make 5 strip units.
Cut 35 segments.

5"

Black A

Black B

Make 5 strip units.
Cut 35 segments.

5"

Green A

Green B

Make 5 strip units.
Cut 35 segments.

3. Join the remaining 2" light strips and 2" B strips to make strip units in three color combinations as shown. Press the seams open or toward the darker fabrics. Cut 35 segments, 2" wide, from the strip units of each color combination.

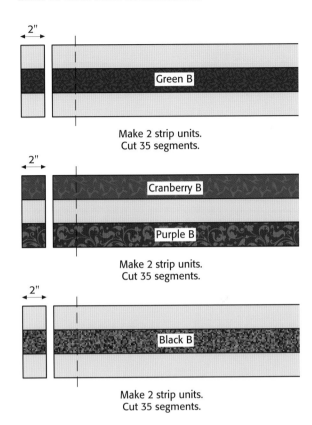

2"

Green B

Make 2 strip units.
Cut 35 segments.

2"

Cranberry B

Purple B

Make 2 strip units.
Cut 35 segments.

2"

Black B

Make 2 strip units.
Cut 35 segments.

4. Join the 2" segments you cut in step 3 to make 35 nine-patch units *exactly* as shown. Note that the cranberry is on the top, the purple is on the bottom, the black is on the left, and the green is on the right. Press the seams open or toward the center segments.

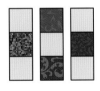

Make 35.

5. Join the green and black segments from step 2 and the nine-patch units from step 4 to make 35 units *exactly* as shown. Press the seams open or away from the nine-patch units.

Make 35.

6. Join the cranberry and green half-square-triangle units from step 1 and the purple segments from step 2 to make 35 units *exactly* as shown. Press the seams open or toward the strip-unit segments.

Make 35.

7. Join the black and purple half-square-triangle units from step 1 and the cranberry segments from step 2 to make 35 units *exactly* as shown. Press the seams open or toward the strip-unit segments.

Make 35.

8. Join the step 5, 6, and 7 units to make 35 blocks *exactly* as shown. Press the seams open or toward the center sections of the blocks.

Make 35.

Assembling the Quilt Top

1. Join the blocks to make seven horizontal rows, each containing five blocks, as shown. Note that the blocks should be arranged so that all of the cranberry half-square triangles are at the upper left. Press the seams in opposite directions from row to row.

2. Join the rows. Press the seams however you wish.

Adding the Border Strips

This quilt has side borders only (see the photo on page 45).

1. Sew the 4" black strips together end to end to make a single long strip; press the seams open. Measure the length of the quilt through the center, from raw edge to raw edge. From the long black strip, cut two border strips to the length measured and join them to the sides of the quilt, matching the ends and centers and easing the edges to fit. Press the seams toward the border.

2. Repeat step 1 with the 4" purple, green, and cranberry strips, staggering the seams when you join the strips to the quilt.

Finishing the Quilt

For detailed instructions on finishing techniques, see "Finishing Your Quilt" on page 84.

1. Divide the backing fabric crosswise into three equal panels. Remove the selvages and join the panels with a ½" seam to make a single, large backing piece. Press the seams open.

2. Layer the quilt top with batting and backing. Baste the layers together.

3. Hand or machine quilt as desired.

4. Prepare and sew the 2½"-wide binding strips to the quilt.

Four Square

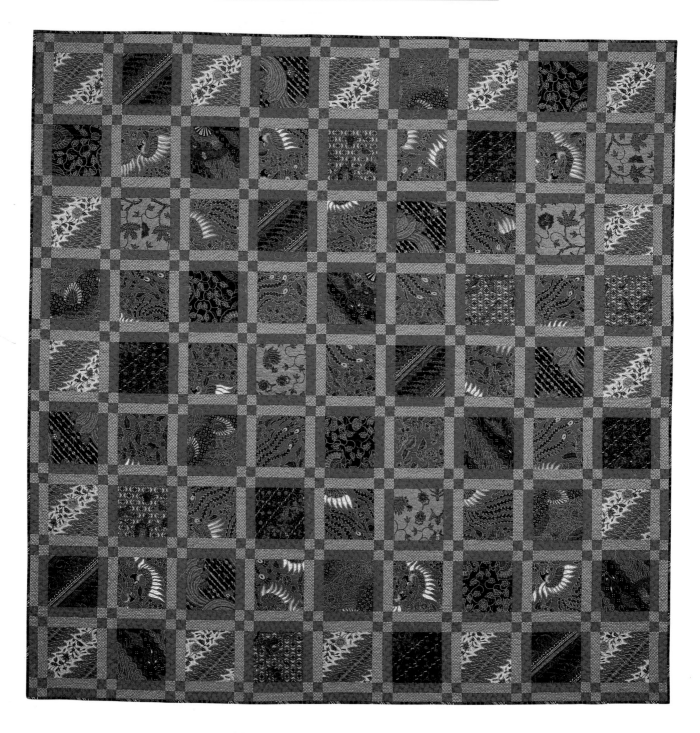

Pieced by Judy Dafoe Hopkins. Quilted by Carol Parks.

Finished quilt size: 97½" x 97½"

Materials

Yardages are based on 42"-wide fabric.

2⅞ yards of red A print for sashing

2⅞ yards of caramel print for sashing

1 strip *exactly* 8" wide and at least 42" long *each* of 8 assorted caramel-and-black prints for squares

1⅜ yards of red B print for squares

1⅛ yards of red C print for squares

9⅝ yards of fabric for backing

⅞ yard of caramel-and-black print for binding

104" x 104" piece of batting

Cutting

All measurements include ¼"-wide seam allowances.

From the red A print, cut:

• 46 selvage-to-selvage strips, 2" wide

From the caramel print, cut:

• 46 selvage-to-selvage strips, 2" wide

From the red B print, cut:

• 5 selvage-to-selvage strips, 8" wide. From these strips, cut 25 squares, 8" x 8".

From the red C print, cut:

• 4 selvage-to-selvage strips, 8" wide. From these strips, cut 16 squares, 8" x 8".

From *each* of the 8 assorted caramel-and-black strips, cut:

• 5 squares, 8" x 8" (40 total)

From the caramel-and-black print for binding, cut:

• 11 selvage-to-selvage strips, 2½" wide, for binding

Making the Units and Assembling the Quilt Top

This is one of those designs that creates an occasional pressing conundrum no matter what you do. If you press the seams open, you may have difficulty matching seams, and you'll have no "ditch" to stitch in when you reach the quilting stage. If you press to the side, you may have to twist some seams on the back when you assemble the blocks and/or the quilt,

to make them butt together properly for easy joining. You choose.

1. Join the 2" red A strips and the 2" caramel strips to make 46 strip units as shown. Press the seams open or toward the red print. From these strip units, cut 200 segments, 2" wide, and 180 segments, 8" wide, as indicated.

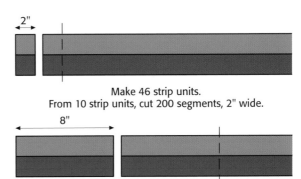

Make 46 strip units.
From 10 strip units, cut 200 segments, 2" wide.

From 36 strip units, cut 180 segments, 8" wide.

2. Join the 2" segments you cut in step 1 to make 100 four-patch units as shown. Press the seams open or however you wish.

Make 100.

3. Join 90 of the four-patch units to 90 of the 8" strip-unit segments from step 1 to make 50 of unit A and 40 of unit B *exactly* as shown. Press the seams open or toward the 8" strips.

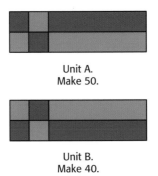

Unit A.
Make 50.

Unit B.
Make 40.

4. Join units A and B from step 3 and the remaining four-patch units to make ten sashing rows (row 1) *exactly* as shown.

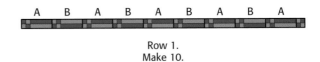

Row 1.
Make 10.

5. Join the remaining 8" strip-unit segments from step 1, the 8" red B and red C squares, and the assorted 8" caramel-and-black squares to make two of row 2, four of row 3, and three of row 4 *exactly* as shown. *Pay particular attention to the orientation of the red A print in the vertical sashing pieces.* Press the seams open or toward the sashing strips.

Row 2.
Make 2.

Row 3.
Make 4.

Row 4.
Make 3.

6. Join the rows, reversing every other sashing row (row 1 and row 1R) as shown below. Press the seams open or however you wish.

Finishing the Quilt

For detailed instructions on finishing techniques, see "Finishing Your Quilt" on page 84.

1. Divide the backing fabric crosswise into three equal panels. Remove the selvages and join the panels with a ½" seam to make a single, large backing piece. Press the seams open.

2. Layer the quilt top with batting and backing. Baste the layers together.

3. Hand or machine quilt as desired.

4. Prepare and sew the 2½"-wide binding strips to the quilt.

Grandmother's Choice

Pieced by Juanita Stark. Quilted by Janet Murdock.

Finished quilt size: 98" x 98"

Finished block size: 10" x 10"

Materials

Yardages are based on 42"-wide fabrics.

5 yards of beige print for block backgrounds, alternate blocks, and seamed inner border

3⅛ yards of pink floral print for outer border*

2¼ yards of blue floral print for block centers and corners, seamed second border, and binding

11" x 17" or 6" x 33" piece *each* of 9 assorted pink, blue, and green prints for blocks

9⅝ yards of fabric for backing. Or, combine fabric left over from making the front of the quilt with other fabrics from your stash to make a pieced backing that's at least 104" x 104".

104" x 104" piece of batting

*Use the same fabric as one of the 9 assorted prints, if you wish.

Cutting

All measurements include ¼"-wide seam allowances.

From the beige print, cut:

- 8 selvage-to-selvage strips, 2⅞" wide. From these strips, cut 100 squares, 2⅞" x 2⅞". Cut the squares once diagonally to make 200 half-square triangles.

- 5 selvage-to-selvage strips, 4½" wide. From 1 of these strips, cut 16 rectangles, 2½" x 4½". Leave the remaining strips uncut.

- 8 selvage-to-selvage strips, 3½" wide, for inner border

From the *length* of the remaining piece of beige print, cut:

- 1 strip, 4½" x about 90". From this strip, cut 34 rectangles, 2½" x 4½". Reserve the remaining fabric for alternate blocks.

From the blue floral print, cut:

- 28 selvage-to-selvage strips, 2½" wide. From 7 of these strips, cut 100 squares, 2½" x 2½". Leave the remaining strips uncut.

From *each* of the 9 assorted pink, blue, and green prints, cut:

- 6 squares, 4⅞" x 4⅞" (54 total). Cut the squares once diagonally to make 12 half-square triangles (108 total). You will use 100 and have 8 left over.

From the *length* of the pink floral print, cut:

- 4 strips, 9½" wide x at least 100" long, for outer border

Making the Blocks

1. Join the 2⅞" beige half-square triangles and the 2½" blue floral squares to make 100 of unit A as shown. Press the seams toward the triangles.

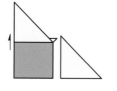

Unit A.
Make 100.

2. Discard four triangles *each* from two of the assorted pink, blue, and green prints (8 total). Join the remaining 4⅞" assorted pink, blue, and green triangles to the units you made in step 1 to make 100 of unit B as shown. Press the seams toward the large triangles.

Unit B.
Make 100.

3. Join the 2½" x 4½" beige rectangles and the units you made in step 2 to make 50 of unit C as shown. Match the fabrics in the large triangles in each unit. Press the seams toward the beige rectangles.

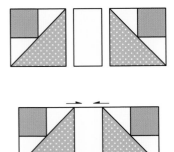

Unit C.
Make 50.

4. Join the 4½" beige strips and two of the 2½" blue floral strips to make two strip units as shown. Press the seams toward the beige print. From these strip units, cut 25 segments, 2½" wide.

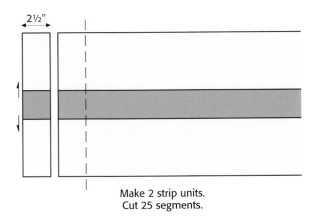

2½"

Make 2 strip units.
Cut 25 segments.

5. Join the units you made in step 3 and the strip-unit segments you cut in step 4 to make 25 blocks. Match the fabrics in the large triangles in each block. Press the seams toward the beige rectangles.

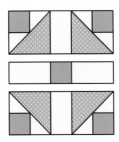
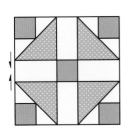

Match the fabrics in the large triangles.

Make 25.

Cutting the Alternate Blocks and Assembling the Quilt Top

1. Measure the pieced blocks through the centers to determine the size to cut the alternate blocks. If your pieced blocks were stitched perfectly, they should measure 10½" square (raw edge to raw edge). However, they might be a little larger or smaller. If the pieced blocks measure several different sizes, determine the average measurement of the blocks.

2. From the remaining beige print, cut three *lengthwise* strips the width determined in step 1. From these strips, cut 24 squares to the proper size (10½" x 10½" if your pieced blocks came out just right).

3. Join the pieced blocks and the alternate blocks to make four of row A and three of row B exactly as shown. Press the seams toward the alternate blocks.

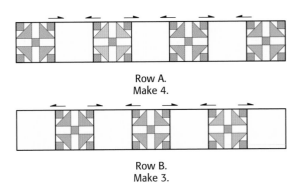

Row A.
Make 4.

Row B.
Make 3.

4. Join the rows as shown. Press the seams however you wish.

Adding the Borders

1. Inner border: Seam the 3½" beige print strips as necessary to make strips long enough to border the quilt. Press the seams open. Measure the length of the quilt through the center, from raw edge to raw edge. Cut two border strips to the length measured and join them to the sides of the quilt, matching the ends and centers and easing the edges to fit. Press the seams toward the border.

2. Measure the width of the quilt through the center, including the border pieces you just added. Cut the remaining two border strips to that measurement and join them to the top and bottom of the quilt as above. Press the seams toward the border.

3. Second border: Seam the 2½" blue floral strips as necessary to make strips long enough to border the quilt. Press the seams open. Measure and add to the quilt as above.

4. Outer border: Measure and add the 9½" pink floral strips to the quilt as above.

Finishing the Quilt

For detailed instructions on finishing techniques, see "Finishing Your Quilt" on page 84.

1. Divide the backing fabric crosswise into three equal panels. Remove the selvages and join the panels with a ½" seam to make a single, large backing piece. Press the seams open.

2. Layer the quilt top with batting and backing. Baste the layers together.

3. Hand or machine quilt as desired.

4. Prepare and sew the remaining 2½"-wide binding strips to the quilt.

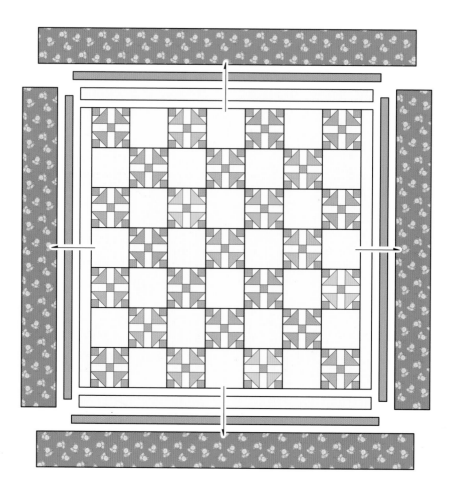

Ladders

Pieced by Jacquelin Carley. Quilted by JoAnn Gruber.

Finished quilt size: 95" x 95"

Materials

Yardages are based on 42"-wide fabrics.

⅓ yard *each* of 16 assorted blue prints for quilt top*

4⅞ yards of floral print for quilt top

1⅜ yards of blue print for quilt top and binding

9¼ yards of fabric for backing

101" x 101" piece of batting

Use the same fabric more than once, if you wish.

Cutting

All measurements include ¼"-wide seam allowances.

From the floral print, cut:

• 53 selvage-to-selvage strips, 3" wide

From *each* of the 16 assorted blue prints, cut:

• 3 selvage-to-selvage strips, 3" wide (48 total). You need 53 strips altogether. The remaining 5 strips will be cut from the blue print for quilt top, below.

From the blue print for quilt top and binding, cut:

• 5 selvage-to-selvage strips, 3" wide

• 10 selvage-to-selvage strips, 2½" wide, for binding

Making the Units

This is one of those designs that creates an occasional pressing conundrum no matter what you do. If you press the seams open, you may have difficulty matching seams, and you'll have no "ditch" to stitch in when you reach the quilting stage. If you press to the side, you may have to twist some seams on the back when you assemble the blocks and/or the quilt, to make them butt together properly for easy joining. The pressing instructions given are what I consider to be the best solution for this quilt.

1. Join three of the 3" floral strips and any three of the 3" blue strips to make three strip units as shown. *Use a different blue print in each strip unit.* Press the seams toward the blue strips. From these strip units, cut 3" and 15½" segments as indicated, for a total of eight 3" segments and five 15½" segments.

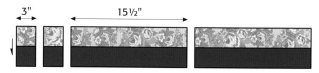

Make 3 strip units.
From 1 strip unit, cut 4 segments, 3" wide, and 1 segment, 15½" wide.

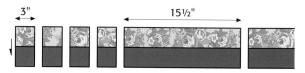

From each of the remaining strip units, cut 2 segments, 3" wide, and 2 segments, 15½" wide.

2. Randomly join the 3" segments you cut in step 1 to make two of unit A and two of unit B as shown. Press the seams open.

Unit A.
Make 2.

Unit B.
Make 2.

3. Join the remaining 3" floral strips and the remaining 3" blue strips to make 25 strip units as shown. Use two different blue strips in each strip unit. Press the seams toward the blue strips. From these strip units, cut 3" and 15½" segments as indicated, for a total of seventy-two 3" segments and forty-five 15½" segments.

Make 25 strip units.
From 2 of the strip units,
cut a *total* of 21 segments, 3" wide.

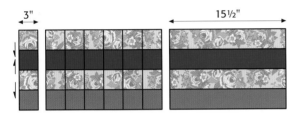

From 1 of the strip units, cut 7 segments,
3" wide, and 1 segment, 15½" wide.

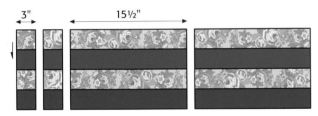

From each of the remaining strip units,
cut 2 segments, 3" wide, and 2 segments, 15½" wide.

4. Randomly join the 3" segments you cut in step 3 to make 18 of unit C and 18 of unit D as shown. Press the seams open.

Unit C.
Make 18.

Unit D.
Make 18.

Assembling the Quilt Top

1. Join the 15½" segments you cut in step 1 and units A and B to make one of section 1 as shown. Combine the fabrics at random. Press the seams toward the 15½" segments.

2. Join the remaining 15½" segments and units C and D to make nine of section 2 as shown. Combine the fabrics at random. Press the seams in opposite directions from section to section.

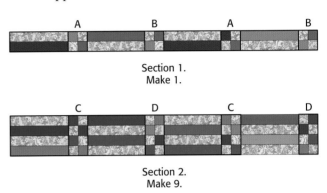

Section 1.
Make 1.

Section 2.
Make 9.

3. Join the sections so the floral and blue strips alternate. Section 1 can be placed anywhere in the sequence. Press the seams however you wish.

Finishing the Quilt

For detailed instructions on finishing techniques, see "Finishing Your Quilt" on page 84.

1. Divide the backing fabric crosswise into three equal panels. Remove the selvages and join the panels with a ½" seam to make a single, large backing piece. Press the seams open.

2. Layer the quilt top with batting and backing. Baste the layers together.

3. Hand or machine quilt as desired.

4. Prepare and sew the 2½"-wide binding strips to the quilt.

McKinley Moods

Pieced and hand quilted by Julie Wilkinson Kimberlin.

Finished quilt size: 98" x 98"

Finished block size: 10" x 10"

Materials

Yardages are based on 42"-wide fabrics.

4⅓ yards of light print for blocks and sashing

4⅓ yards of multicolored print for seamed outer border and binding

1⅝ yards of taupe print for blocks, sashing squares, and seamed inner border

12" x 18" piece *each* of 12 assorted dark prints (greens, blues, reddish violets) for blocks

½ yard of green striped fabric for seamed second border

9⅝ yards of fabric for backing

104" x 104" piece of batting

Cutting

All measurements include ¼"-wide seam allowances.

From the light print, cut:

- 2 selvage-to-selvage strips, 18" wide. From these strips, cut 24 segments, 2½" wide, to make 2½" x 18" strips.

- 9 selvage-to-selvage strips, 4⅞" wide. From these strips, cut 72 squares, 4⅞" x 4⅞". Cut the squares once diagonally to make 144 half-square triangles.

- 8 selvage-to-selvage strips, 2½" wide, for inner border. Reserve the remaining fabric for sashing.

From *each* of the 12 dark prints, cut:

- 4 strips, 2½" x 18" (48 total). From 2 strips of *each* fabric, cut 12 squares, 2½" x 2½" (144 total). Leave the remaining strips uncut.

From the taupe print, cut:

- 1 selvage-to-selvage strip, 9" wide. From this strip, cut 12 segments, 2½" wide, to make 2½" x 9" strips.

- 12 selvage-to-selvage strips, 2⅞" wide. From these strips, cut 144 squares, 2⅞" x 2⅞". Cut the squares once diagonally to make 288 half-square triangles.

- 2 selvage-to-selvage strips, 2½" wide. From these strips, cut 25 squares, 2½" x 2½".

From the green striped fabric, cut:

- 8 selvage-to-selvage strips, 1½" wide, for second border

From the multicolored print, cut:

- 10 selvage-to-selvage strips, 11½" wide, for outer border

- 11 selvage-to-selvage strips, 2½" wide, for binding

Making the Blocks

1. Join two 2½" x 18" light strips and two matching 2½" dark strips to make two strip units as shown. Press the seams toward the dark fabric. From *each* of these strip units, cut three segments, 2½" wide (six total), and one segment, 9" wide (two total), as indicated.

Make 2 strip units using the same dark fabric.

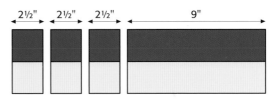

Cut three segments, 2½" wide,
and one segment, 9" wide, from each strip unit.

2. Join the 9" segments you cut in step 1 and a 2½" x 9" taupe strip to make one strip unit. Press the seams away from the taupe print. From this strip unit, cut three segments, 2½" wide.

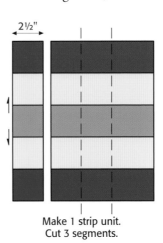

Make 1 strip unit.
Cut 3 segments.

3. Using the same dark print you used above, join 2⅞" taupe half-square triangles and 2½" dark squares to make 12 of unit A. Press the seams toward the squares.

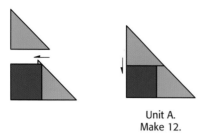

Unit A.
Make 12.

4. Join 4⅞" light half-square triangles to the step 3 units to make 12 of unit B. Press the seams however you wish.

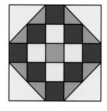

Unit B.
Make 12.

5. Join the strip-unit segments and the B units to make three blocks as shown. Press the seams as indicated.

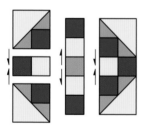

Make 3.

6. Repeat steps 1–5 with the remaining fabrics, making three blocks at a time, for a total of 36 blocks.

Cutting the Sashing and Assembling the Quilt Top

1. Measure the blocks through the centers to determine the size to cut the sashing strips. If your blocks were stitched perfectly, they should measure 10½" square (raw edge to raw edge). However, they might be a little larger or smaller. If the blocks measure several different sizes, determine the average measurement of the blocks.

2. From the remaining light print, cut four selvage-to-selvage strips the width determined in step 1 for the blocks (10½" if your blocks came out perfectly). From these strips, cut 60 rectangles, 2½" wide.

3. Join the blocks, the sashing rectangles, and the 2½" taupe squares to make six block rows and five sashing rows as shown. If you used average measurements, you can take care of any minor discrepancies by easing either the blocks or the sashing strips as you sew. Press the seams toward the sashing rectangles.

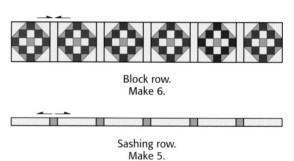

Block row.
Make 6.

Sashing row.
Make 5.

4. Join the rows as shown. Press the seams however you wish.

Adding the Borders

1. Inner border: Seam the 2½" light strips as necessary to make strips long enough to border the quilt. Press the seams open. Measure the length of the quilt through the center, from raw edge to raw edge. Cut two border strips to the length measured and join them to the sides of the quilt, matching the ends and centers and easing the edges to fit. Press the seams toward the border.

2. Measure the width of the quilt through the center, including the border pieces you just added. Cut the remaining two border strips to that measurement and join them to the top and bottom of the quilt as above. Press the seams toward the border.

3. Repeat steps 1 and 2 with the 1½" strips of green striped fabric for the second border.

4. Repeat steps 1 and 2 with the 11½" multicolored print strips for the outer border.

Finishing the Quilt

For detailed instructions on finishing techniques, see "Finishing Your Quilt" on page 84.

1. Divide the backing fabric crosswise into three equal panels. Remove the selvages and join the panels with a ½" seam to make a single, large backing piece. Press the seams open.

2. Layer the quilt top with batting and backing. Baste the layers together.

3. Hand or machine quilt as desired.

4. Prepare and sew the 2½"-wide binding strips to the quilt.

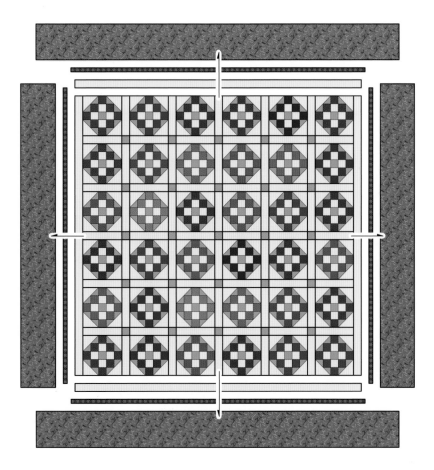

Millennium

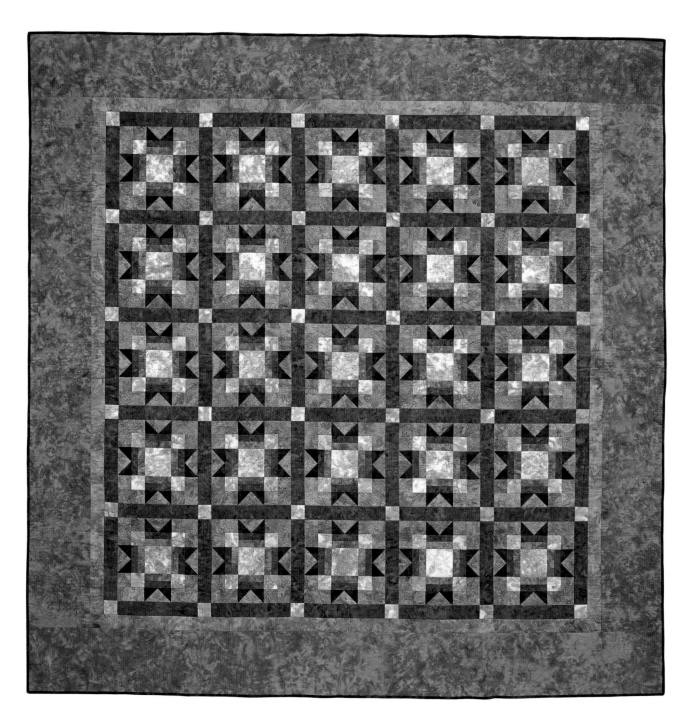

Pieced by Michele A. Hall. Quilted by Craig "Grumpy" Campbell.

Finished quilt size: 94" x 94"

Finished block size: 12" x 12"

Materials

Yardages are based on 42"-wide fabrics. The four blue prints should form a smooth gradation from light to dark. Tape a snip of each of these fabrics to an index card and label the snips for reference during the cutting and assembly process.

1⅓ yards of light blue print for blocks and sashing squares

3⅝ yards of medium blue print for blocks and outer border

2¼ yards of dark-medium blue print for blocks and sashing pieces

1½ yards of dark blue print for blocks and binding

2⅞ yards of medium green print for blocks and seamed inner border

9¼ yards of fabric for backing

100" x 100" piece of batting

Cutting

All measurements include ¼"-wide seam allowances.

From the dark blue print, cut:

- 8 selvage-to-selvage strips, 2⅞" wide. From these strips, cut 100 squares, 2⅞" x 2⅞". Cut the squares once diagonally to make 200 half-square triangles.

- 10 selvage-to-selvage strips, 2½" wide, for binding

From the medium green print, cut:

- 4 selvage-to-selvage strips, 5¼" wide. From these strips, cut 25 squares, 5¼" x 5¼". Cut the squares twice diagonally to make 100 quarter-square triangles.

- 7 selvage-to-selvage strips, 4½" wide. From these strips, cut 100 rectangles, 2½" x 4½".

- 15 selvage-to-selvage strips, 2½" wide (7 strips for blocks, 8 strips for inner border)

From the light blue print, cut:

- 4 selvage-to-selvage strips, 4½" wide. From these strips, cut 25 squares, 4½" x 4½".

- 10 selvage-to-selvage strips, 2½" wide. From 3 of these strips, cut 36 squares, 2½" x 2½". Leave the remaining strips uncut.

From the medium blue print, cut:

- 13 selvage-to-selvage strips, 1½" wide

From the *length* of the remaining medium blue print, cut:

- 4 strips, 9½" x about 97", for outer border

From the dark-medium blue print, cut:

- 13 selvage-to-selvage strips, 1½" wide. Reserve the remaining fabric for sashing.

Making the Blocks

1. Join the 2⅞" dark blue half-square triangles and the 5¼" medium green quarter-square triangles to make 100 flying-geese units. (See "Stitching Tips for Flying-Geese Units" on page 14.) Press the seams toward the dark blue triangles.

Flying-geese unit.
Make 100.

2. Join the 2½" light blue strips and the 2½" medium green strips to make seven strip units as shown. Press the seams toward the medium green print. From these strip units, cut 100 segments, 2½" wide.

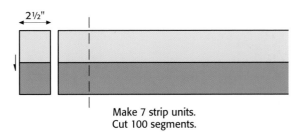

Make 7 strip units.
Cut 100 segments.

3. Join the 2½" x 4½" medium green rectangles to the strip-unit segments you cut in step 2 to make 100 of unit A. Press the seams toward the rectangles.

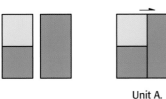

Unit A.
Make 100.

4. Join the 1½" medium blue strips and the 1½" dark-medium blue strips to make 13 strip units as shown. Press the seams toward the medium blue print. From these strip units, cut 100 segments, 4½" wide.

4½"

Make 13 strip units.
Cut 100 segments.

5. Join the strip-unit segments you cut in step 4 and the flying-geese units from step 1 to make 100 of unit B *exactly* as shown. Press the seams toward the dark-medium blue strips.

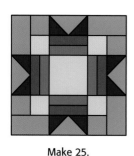

Unit B.
Make 100.

6. Join units A and B from the previous steps and the 4½" light blue squares to make 25 blocks as shown. Press the seams as indicated.

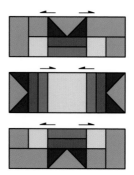

Make 25.

Cutting the Sashing and Assembling the Quilt Top

1. Measure the blocks through the centers to determine the size to cut the sashing strips. If your blocks were stitched perfectly, they should measure 12½" square (raw edge to raw edge). However, they might be a little larger or smaller. If the blocks measure several different sizes, determine the average measurement of the blocks.

2. From the remaining dark-medium blue print, cut four selvage-to-selvage strips the width determined in step 1. From these strips, cut 60 sashing pieces, 2½" wide.

3. Join the blocks, the sashing pieces, and the 2½" light blue squares to make six sashing rows and five block rows as shown. If you used average measurements, you can take care of any minor discrepancies by easing either the blocks or the sashing strips as you sew. Press the seams toward the sashing pieces.

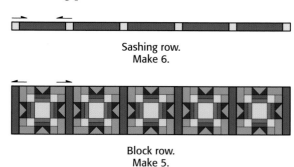

Sashing row.
Make 6.

Block row.
Make 5.

4. Join the rows as shown. Press the seams however you wish.

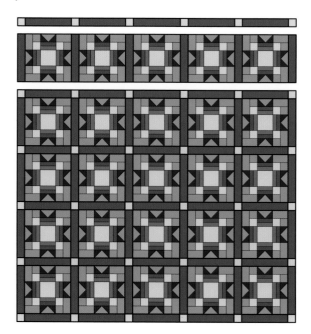

Adding the Borders

1. Seam the 2½" medium green strips as necessary to make strips long enough to border the quilt; press the seams open. Measure the length of the quilt through the center, from raw edge to raw edge. Cut two border strips to the length measured and join them to the sides of the quilt, matching the ends and centers and easing the edges to fit. Press the seams toward the border.

2. Measure the width of the quilt through the center, including the border pieces you just added. Cut the remaining two border strips to that measurement and join them to the top and bottom of the quilt as above. Press the seams toward the border.

3. Repeat steps 1 and 2 with the 9½" medium blue strips for the outer border.

Finishing the Quilt

For detailed instructions on finishing techniques, see "Finishing Your Quilt" on page 84.

1. Divide the backing fabric crosswise into three equal panels. Remove the selvages and join the panels with a ½" seam to make a single, large backing piece. Press the seams open.

2. Layer the quilt top with batting and backing. Baste the layers together.

3. Hand or machine quilt as desired.

4. Prepare and sew the 2½"-wide binding strips to the quilt.

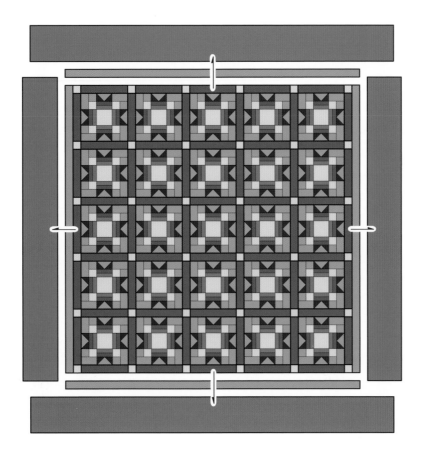

Nine Patch Strippy

Pieced by Judy DeLano. Quilted by Carol Parks.

Finished quilt size: 99" x 99"

Finished block size: 9" x 9"

Materials

Yardages are based on 42"-wide fabrics.

6⅓ yards of large-scale red print for vertical bars and binding

⅜ yard *each* of 11 assorted light gold prints for block corners*

1½ yards of gold-and-red print for blocks

⅞ yard of red print for blocks

⅔ yard of green print for blocks

9⅝ yards of fabric for backing

105" x 105" piece of batting

Use the same fabric more than once, if you wish.

Cutting

All measurements include ¼"-wide seam allowances.

From the gold-and-red print, cut:

• 18 selvage-to-selvage strips, 2⅝" wide

From the red print, cut:

• 10 selvage-to-selvage strips, 2⅝" wide

From the green print, cut:

• 8 selvage-to-selvage strips, 2⅝" wide

From *each* of the 11 assorted light gold prints, cut:

• 2 strips, 5⅜" wide x about 29" long (22 total). Cut 5 squares, 5⅜" x 5⅜", from *each* strip (110 total). Cut the squares once diagonally to make 220 half-square triangles.

Large-scale red print:

Divide the large-scale red print crosswise into 2 equal panels.

• From the *length* of 1 of these panels, cut 4 strips, 9½" wide x about 104" long, for vertical bars

• From the *length* of the remaining panel, cut:

    2 strips, 9½" wide x about 104" long, for vertical bars

    4 strips, 2½" wide x about 104" long, for binding

Using Leftover Fabric

Use any leftover fabric as part of a pieced backing or to make or trim throw pillows, pillowcases, or pillow shams. (See "Making Pillowcases and Shams" on page 90.)

Making the Blocks

1. Join the 2⅝" gold-and-red print strips, green print strips, and red print strips to make strip units as shown. Press the seams toward the red strips. Cut the number of 2⅝"-wide segments indicated from each strip unit.

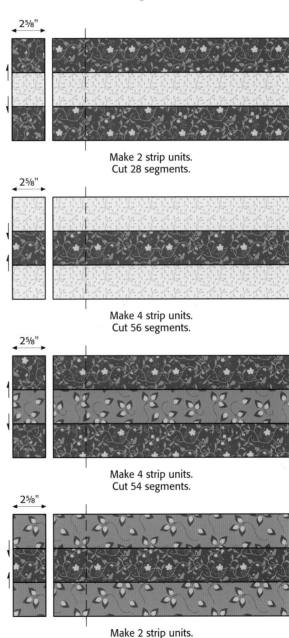

2⅝"

Make 2 strip units.
Cut 28 segments.

2⅝"

Make 4 strip units.
Cut 56 segments.

2⅝"

Make 4 strip units.
Cut 54 segments.

2⅝"

Make 2 strip units.
Cut 27 segments.

2. Join the segments you cut in step 1 to make 28 of unit A and 27 of unit B. Press the seams however you wish.

 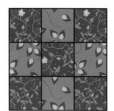

Unit A.
Make 28.

Unit B.
Make 27.

3. Join 5⅜" assorted gold half-square triangles to each of the units you made in step 2 to make 28 of block A and 27 of block B. (See "Stitching Tips for Square-in-a-Square Units" on page 13.) Use the same fabric in all four corners of each block. Press the seams toward the triangles.

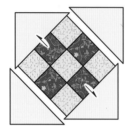 

Block A.
Make 28.

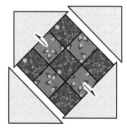 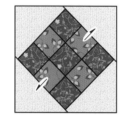

Block B.
Make 27.

Use the same fabric in all four corners of each block.

Assembling the Quilt Top

1. Join the blocks to make three of row A and two of row B, alternating block A and block B in each row as shown. Each row contains 11 blocks. Note that the A rows begin and end with block A; the B rows begin and end with block B. Press the seams however you wish.

2. Measure the lengths of rows A and B through the centers, from raw edge to raw edge; find the average of these measurements. Cut the 9½" large-scale red print strips to this average measurement. Join the strips and the pieced rows as shown in the photo on page 68, matching the ends and centers and easing the edges to fit. Press the seams toward the red print strips.

Row A.
Make 3.

Row B.
Make 2.

Finishing the Quilt

For detailed instructions on finishing techniques, see "Finishing Your Quilt" on page 84.

1. Divide the backing fabric crosswise into three equal panels. Remove the selvages and join the panels with a ½" seam to make a single, large backing piece. Press the seams open.

2. Layer the quilt top with batting and backing. Baste the layers together.

3. Hand or machine quilt as desired.

4. Prepare and sew the 2½"-wide binding strips to the quilt.

Pieced by Judy Dafoe Hopkins. Quilted by Sandra K. Carr.

Finished quilt size: 98¼" x 97¾"

Materials

Yardages are based on 42"-wide fabrics.

6¾ yards of tropical print for blocks, seamed border, and binding

4⅝ yards of striped fabric for sashing pieces

1⅜ yards of yellow print for sashing squares and border corner squares

9⅝ yards of fabric for backing

104" x 104" piece of batting

Cutting

All measurements include ¼"-wide seam allowances.

From the tropical print, cut:

- 6 selvage-to-selvage strips, 4½" wide
- 6 selvage-to-selvage strips, 5½" wide
- 6 selvage-to-selvage strips, 6½" wide
- 6 selvage-to-selvage strips, 7½" wide
- 10 selvage-to-selvage strips, 5" wide, for border
- 11 selvage-to-selvage strips, 2½" wide, for binding

From the striped fabric, cut:

- 26 selvage-to-selvage strips, 2¼" wide

Remaining striped fabric:

Divide the remaining striped fabric crosswise into 2 equal panels, each at least 45" long.

- From the *length* of 1 of these panels, cut:

    2 strips, 4½" x 45"

    2 strips, 5½" x 45"

    2 strips, 6½" x 45"

    1 strip, 7½" x 45"

- From the *length* of the remaining panel, cut 2 strips, 7½" x 45"

From the *length* of the yellow print, cut:

- 10 strips, 2¼" wide x at least 45" long

From the remaining yellow print, cut:

- 4 squares, 5" x 5", for border corners

> ### *Using Leftover Fabric*
> *Use any leftover fabric as part of a pieced backing or to make or trim throw pillows, pillowcases, or pillow shams. (See "Making Pillowcases and Shams" on page 90.)*

Making the Units and Assembling the Quilt Top

1. Join the 2¼" striped strips and the 4½", 5½", 6½", and 7½" tropical print strips to make strip units as shown. Press the seams toward the striped fabric. Cut the number of 7½"-wide segments indicated from each strip unit.

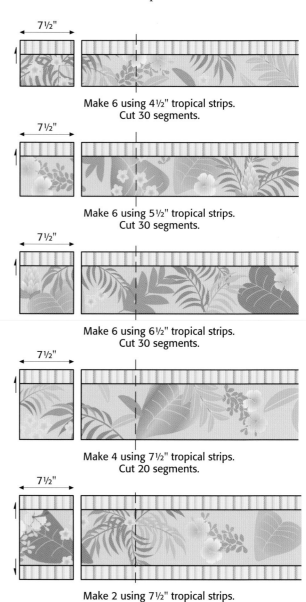

Make 6 using 4½" tropical strips.
Cut 30 segments.

Make 6 using 5½" tropical strips.
Cut 30 segments.

Make 6 using 6½" tropical strips.
Cut 30 segments.

Make 4 using 7½" tropical strips.
Cut 20 segments.

Make 2 using 7½" tropical strips.
Cut 10 segments.

2. Join the 2¼" yellow strips and the 4½", 5½", 6½", and 7½" strips cut from the length of the striped fabric to make strip units as shown. Press the seams toward the striped fabric. Cut the number of 2¼"-wide segments indicated from each strip unit.

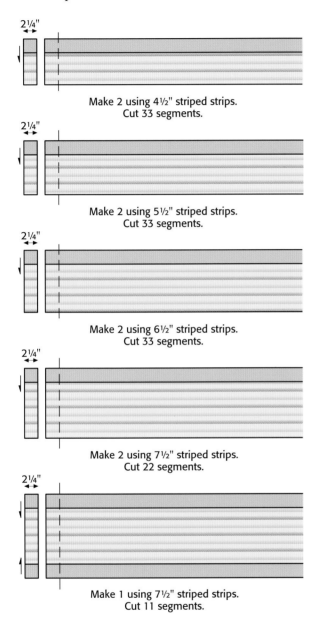

2¼"

Make 2 using 4½" striped strips.
Cut 33 segments.

2¼"

Make 2 using 5½" striped strips.
Cut 33 segments.

2¼"

Make 2 using 6½" striped strips.
Cut 33 segments.

2¼"

Make 2 using 7½" striped strips.
Cut 22 segments.

2¼"

Make 1 using 7½" striped strips.
Cut 11 segments.

3. Join the segments you cut in the previous steps to make 11 of row A and 10 of row B as shown above right. Press the seams toward the striped fabric. Note that each row contains three 4½"

units, three 5½" units, three 6½" units, and three 7½" units.

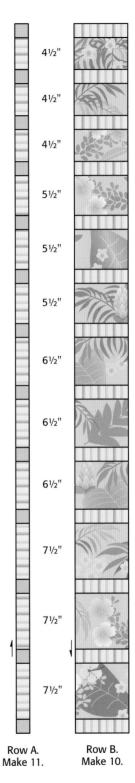

4½"

4½"

4½"

5½"

5½"

5½"

6½"

6½"

6½"

7½"

7½"

7½"

Row A.
Make 11.

Row B.
Make 10.

4. Join the rows as shown in the photo on page 71. Press the seams however you wish.

Adding the Border

1. Seam the 5" tropical print strips as necessary to make strips long enough to border the quilt; press the seams open. Measure the length and width of the quilt through the center, from raw edge to raw edge.

   Note: This quilt measures slightly wider than it does long, so your lengthwise and crosswise measurements will differ.

2. Cut two border strips to the lengthwise measurement and join them to the sides of the quilt, matching the ends and centers and easing the edges to fit. Press the seams toward the border.

3. Cut the remaining two border strips to the original crosswise measurement. Join the 5" yellow squares to the ends of the strips and join these pieced strips to the top and bottom of the quilt, matching the ends, seams, and centers, and easing as necessary. Press the seams toward the border.

Finishing the Quilt

For detailed instructions on finishing techniques, see "Finishing Your Quilt" on page 84.

1. Divide the backing fabric crosswise into three equal panels. Remove the selvages and join the panels with a ½" seam to make a single, large backing piece. Press the seams open.

2. Layer the quilt top with batting and backing. Baste the layers together.

3. Hand or machine quilt as desired.

4. Prepare and sew the 2½"-wide binding strips to the quilt.

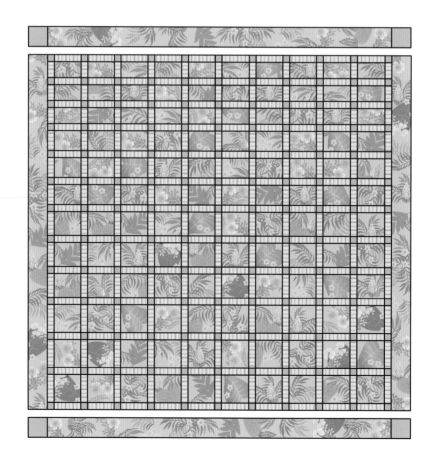

Quartered Log Cabin

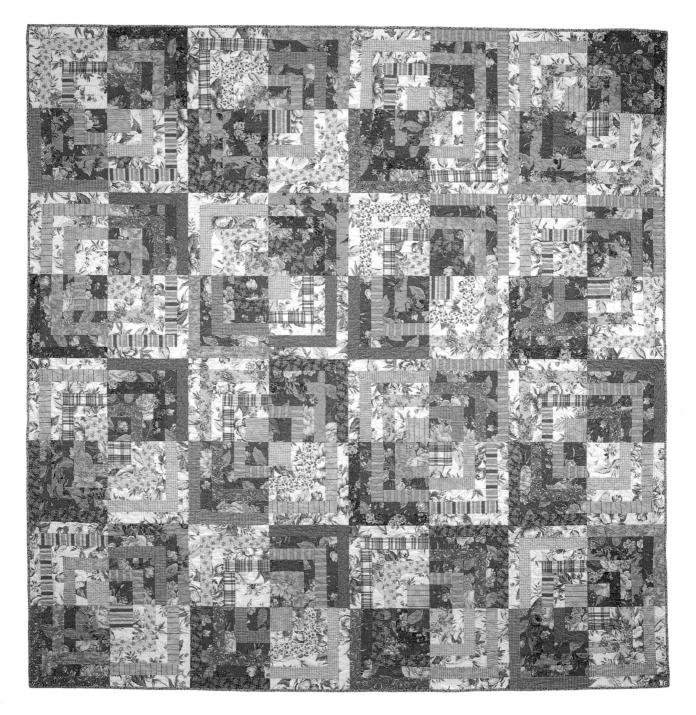

Pieced by Terri Shinn. Quilted by Judy Irish.

Finished quilt size: 98" x 98"

Finished block size: 24½" x 24½"

Materials

Yardages are based on 42"-wide fabrics. Because of the stitch-and-trim sewing method used for the blocks, extra fabric has been allowed.

⅝ yard *each* of 8 assorted red and/or yellow prints, plaids, and striped fabrics for unit A

⅝ yard *each* of 8 assorted green prints, plaids, and striped fabrics for unit B

3¾ yards of light floral print for unit A

3 yards of red floral print for unit B*

⅞ yard of green floral print for binding

9⅝ yards of fabric for backing

104" x 104" piece of batting

The red floral print in the pictured quilt was used wrong side up to achieve a softer look.

Cutting

All measurements include ¼"-wide seam allowances.

From the light floral print, cut:

• 49 selvage-to-selvage strips, 2¼" wide

From *each* of the 8 assorted red and/or yellow prints, plaids, and striped fabrics, cut:

• 5 selvage-to-selvage strips, 2¼" wide (40 total)

• 4 squares, 4" x 4" (32 total)

From the red floral print, cut:

• 4 selvage-to-selvage strips, 4" wide. From these strips, cut 32 squares, 4" x 4".

• 33 selvage-to-selvage strips, 2¼" wide

From *each* of the 8 green prints, cut:

• 7 selvage-to-selvage strips, 2¼" wide (56 total)

From the green floral print, cut:

• 11 selvage-to-selvage strips, 2½" wide, for binding

Using Leftover Fabric

Use any leftover fabric as part of a pieced backing or to make or trim throw pillows, pillowcases, or pillow shams. (See "Making Pillowcases and Shams" on page 90.)

Making the Blocks

General Instructions: To make the units for each block, you'll sew long strips to the squares and to the resulting units, trim the strips even with the edges of the pieces to which the strips have been joined, and then press the seams, as shown.

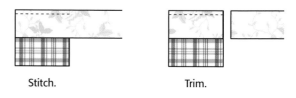

Stitch.   Trim.

Press.

1. Make 32 A units. Following the general instructions above, join 2¼" light floral strips to the left sides and tops of the assorted 4" red and/or yellow print, plaid, and striped squares. Trim after each seam is sewn. Press the seams toward the light floral.

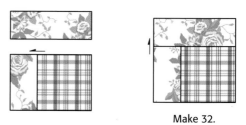

Make 32.

2. Continue to add strips to the left sides and tops of these units, alternating red and/or yellow strips and light floral strips and ending with light floral strips. Use three different red and/or yellow fabrics in each unit, but use matching strips to

form the L shapes. Trim after each seam is sewn. Always press the seams toward the light floral.

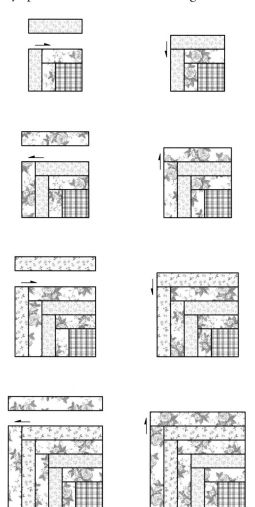

Unit A.
Make 32.

3. Make 32 B units: Following the general instructions above, join 2¼" green print strips to the right sides and tops of the 4" red floral squares. Use each of the eight green prints four times, but use the same green print to form the L shapes in each unit. Trim after each seam is sewn. Press the seams toward the red floral squares.

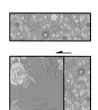 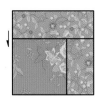

Make 32.

4. Continue to add strips to the right sides and tops of these units, alternating red floral and green print strips and ending with green strips. Use three different green prints in each unit, but use matching strips to form the L shapes. Trim after each strip is sewn. Always press the seams toward the red floral.

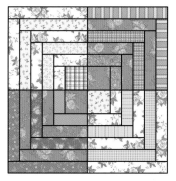

Unit B.
Make 32.

5. Join units A and B to make 16 blocks as shown. Combine the fabrics at random. Press the seams however you wish.

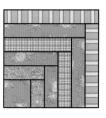

Make 16.

Assembling the Quilt Top

1. Join the blocks to make four horizontal rows, each containing four blocks. Press the seams in opposite directions from row to row.

2. Join the rows as shown in the photo on page 75. Press the seams however you wish.

Finishing the Quilt

For detailed instructions on finishing techniques, see "Finishing Your Quilt" on page 84.

1. Divide the backing fabric crosswise into three equal panels. Remove the selvages and join the panels with a ½" seam to make a single, large backing piece. Press the seams open.

2. Layer the quilt top with batting and backing. Baste the layers together.

3. Hand or machine quilt as desired.

4. Prepare and sew the 2½"-wide binding strips to the quilt.

String Cross

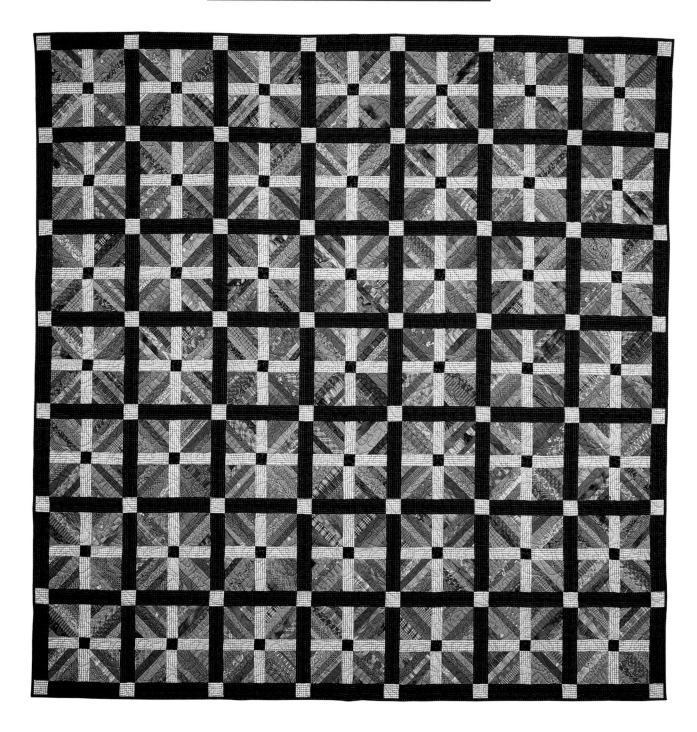

Pieced by Judy Dafoe Hopkins and Rianne Campbell. Quilted by Sandra K. Carr.

Finished quilt size: 96¾" x 96¾"

Finished block size: 11¼" x 11¼"

Materials

Yardages are based on 42"-wide fabrics.

Approximately 9 yards *total* of assorted scraps and strips for blocks*

3¾ yards of dark blue plaid for sashing and binding

2⅜ yards of tan gingham for blocks

⅜ yard of brown print for blocks

9½ yards of fabric for backing

103" x 103" piece of batting

You can supplement your scraps by cutting strips and wedges ranging from 1" to 1¾" wide from yardage purchased specifically for the quilt or from your stash.

Cutting

All measurements include ¼"-wide seam allowances.

From the tan gingham, cut:

- 12 selvage-to-selvage strips, 5¼" wide. From 6 of these strips, cut 98 rectangles, 2¼" x 5¼". Leave the remaining strips uncut.

- 5 selvage-to-selvage strips, 2¾" wide. From 1 of these strips, cut 8 squares, 2¾" x 2¾". Leave the remaining strips uncut.

From the brown print, cut:

- 3 selvage-to-selvage strips, 2¼" wide

From the dark blue plaid, cut:

- 8 selvage-to-selvage strips, 11¾" wide. From 4 of these strips, cut 56 rectangles, 2¾" x 11¾". Leave the remaining strips uncut.

- 11 selvage-to-selvage strips, 2½" wide, for binding

Making the Blocks and Assembling the Quilt Top

1. Press your scraps and cut them into strips or wedges ranging from 1" to 1¾" wide. Use the assorted scraps and strips to make 196 strip-pieced squares, 5¼" x 5¼".

You can combine fabrics at random to make 196 pieces of "scrap fabric" about 6" square and cut a 5¼" square from each piece, **OR** you can use longer strips (join short pieces end to end as necessary) to make 22 pieces of scrap fabric about 18" square, and cut nine 5¼" squares from each piece.

Note: It's not necessary to piece these "scrap fabrics" on foundation fabric, but you can if you wish. If you use the 18"-square method and choose to piece on foundations, you'll need 6⅛ yards of muslin or "waste" fabric; cut 22 foundation squares, 18" x 18".

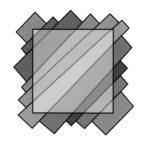
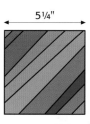

First option:
make 196 squares,
1 at a time.

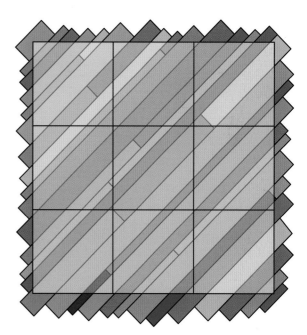

Second option: make 22 large scrap-fabric
pieces and cut 9 squares from each.

2. Join the 5¼" tan gingham strips and the 2¼" brown print strips to make three strip units as shown. Press the seams toward the gingham strips. From these strip units, cut 49 segments, 2¼" wide.

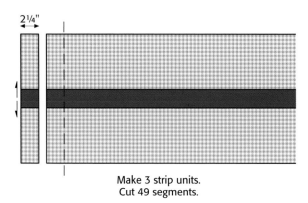

Make 3 strip units.
Cut 49 segments.

3. Join the 5¼" strip-pieced squares, the 2¼" x 5¼" tan gingham rectangles, and the segments from step 2 to make 49 blocks. *Be sure the diagonal seams in the strip-pieced squares are running from the outside corners of the blocks toward the centers of the blocks as shown.* Press the seams toward the gingham rectangles.

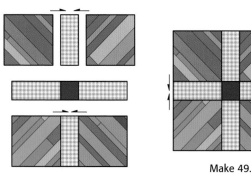

Make 49.

4. Join the 2¾" tan gingham strips and the 11¾" blue plaid strips to make four strip units. Press

the seams toward the blue plaid strips. From these strip units, cut 56 segments, 2¾" wide.

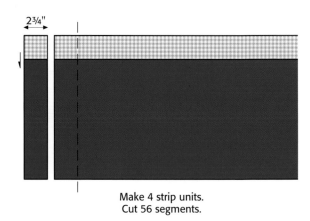

Make 4 strip units.
Cut 56 segments.

5. Join the blocks, the segments from step 4, the 2¾" x 11¾" blue plaid rectangles, and the 2¾" tan gingham squares to make eight sashing rows and seven block rows as shown. Press the seams toward the blue plaid.

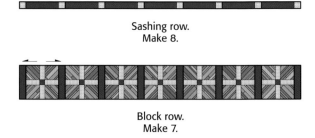

Sashing row.
Make 8.

Block row.
Make 7.

6. Join the rows as shown in the photo on page 78. Press the seams however you wish.

Finishing the Quilt

For detailed instructions on finishing techniques, see "Finishing Your Quilt" on page 84.

1. Divide the backing fabric crosswise into three equal panels. Remove the selvages and join the panels with a ½" seam to make a single, large backing piece. Press the seams open.

2. Layer the quilt top with batting and backing. Baste the layers together.

3. Hand or machine quilt as desired.

4. Prepare and sew the 2½"-wide binding strips to the quilt.

Waterfalls

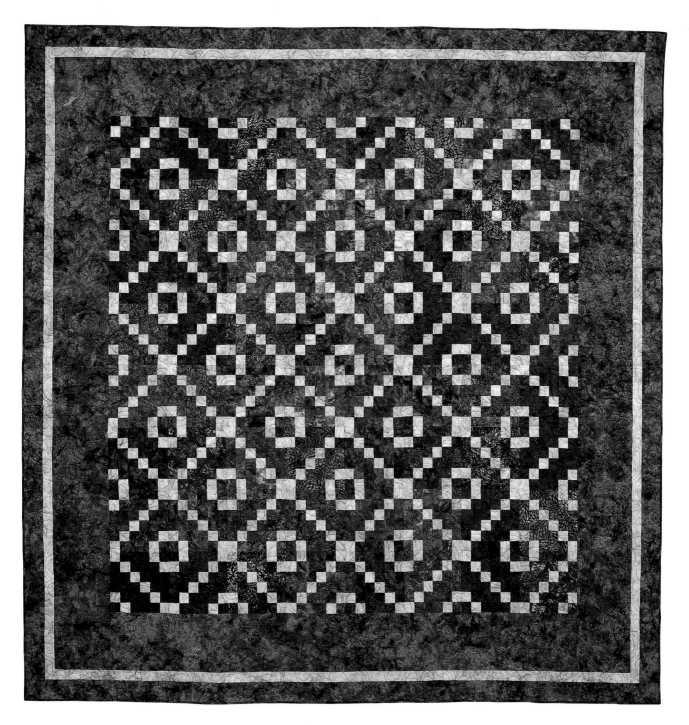

Pieced by Martha M. Morris. Quilted by Tracey Dukowitz.

Finished quilt size: 98" x 98"

Finished block size: 9" x 9"

Materials

Yardages are based on 42"-wide fabrics.

⅜ yard *each* of 16 assorted dark prints (blues, greens, and purples) for blocks

4¾ yards of multicolored print for inner border, seamed outer border, and binding*

3⅛ yards of cream print for blocks and seamed second border

9⅝ yards of fabric for backing

104" x 104" piece of batting

*Use the same fabric as 1 of the assorted dark prints, if you wish.

Cutting

All measurements include ¼"-wide seam allowances.

From *each* of the 16 assorted dark prints, cut:

- 2 selvage-to-selvage strips, 5" wide (32 total)
- 1 selvage-to-selvage strip, 2" wide (16 total)

From the cream print, cut:

- 50 selvage-to-selvage strips, 2" wide. Set 10 of the strips aside for the second border.
- Cut 8 of the strips in half widthwise to make 16 strips, 2" x about 21"

From the multicolored print, cut:

- 10 selvage-to-selvage strips, 3½" wide, for outer border
- 11 selvage-to-selvage strips, 2½" wide, for binding

From the *length* of the remaining multicolored print, cut:

- 4 strips, 9" wide x at least 92" long, for inner border

Using Leftover Fabric

Use any leftover fabric as part of a pieced backing or to make or trim throw pillows, pillowcases, or pillow shams. (See "Making Pillowcases and Shams" on page 90.)

Making the Blocks

This is one of those designs that creates an occasional pressing conundrum no matter what you do. If you press the seams open, you may have difficulty matching seams, and you'll have no "ditch" to stitch in when you reach the quilting stage. If you press to the side, you may have to twist some seams on the back when you assemble the blocks and/or the quilt, to make them butt together properly for easy joining. You choose.

1. Cut *one* 5" strip of *each* of the assorted dark prints in half crosswise to make two strips, 5" x about 21". Trim one 5" x about 21" strip to 3½" wide, as shown. You'll have a total of 16 strips, 5" x about 21", and 16 strips, 3½" x about 21".

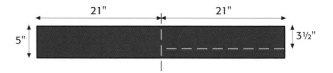

2. Using the *selvage-to-selvage strips,* join two 2" cream strips, a 2" dark strip, and a matching 5" dark strip to make one strip unit as shown. Press the seams open or toward the dark prints. From this strip unit, cut 16 segments, 2" wide.

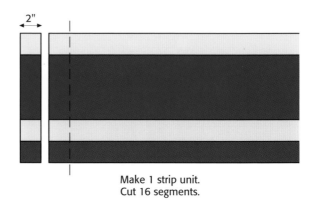

Make 1 strip unit.
Cut 16 segments.

3. Using the same dark print as in step 1, join a 3½" x about 21" dark strip, a 2" x about 21" cream strip, and a 5" x about 21" dark strip to make one strip unit, as shown on the facing page.

Press the seams open or toward the dark prints. From this strip unit, cut eight segments, 2" wide.

2"

Make 1 strip unit.
Cut 8 segments.

4. Join the step 2 and step 3 segments to make four blocks as shown. Press the seams open or all one direction.

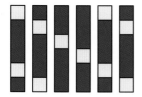

Make 4.

5. Repeat steps 1–3 with the remaining 2", 3½", and 5" dark strips and the 2" cream strips to make a total of 64 blocks. Now that you know what you're doing, you can work with several combinations of cream and dark fabrics at once. *Just remember that the finished blocks should each contain just two fabrics—the cream print and one of the assorted dark prints.*

Assembling the Quilt Top

1. Join the blocks to make 16 four-block units *exactly* as shown. Combine the fabrics at random. Press the seams open or to one side.

Make 16.

2. Join the blocks to make four horizontal rows, each containing four blocks. Press the seams in opposite directions from row to row.

3. Join the rows as shown in the photo on page 81. Press the seams however you wish.

Adding the Borders

1. For the inner border, measure the length of the quilt through the center, from raw edge to raw edge. Cut two of the 9" multicolored border strips to the length measured and join them to the sides of the quilt, matching the ends and centers and easing the edges to fit. Press the seams toward the border.

2. Measure the width of the quilt through the center, including the border pieces you just added. Cut the remaining two 9" multicolored border strips to that measurement and join them to the top and bottom of the quilt as above. Press the seams toward the border.

3. For the second border, seam the remaining 2" cream strips as necessary to make strips long enough to border the quilt; press the seams open. Measure and add to the quilt as above.

4. Repeat step 3 with the 3½" multicolored strips for the outer border.

Finishing the Quilt

For detailed instructions on finishing techniques, see "Finishing Your Quilt" on page 84.

1. Divide the backing fabric crosswise into three equal panels. Remove the selvages and join the panels with a ½" seam to make a single, large backing piece. Press the seams open.

2. Layer the quilt top with batting and backing. Baste the layers together.

3. Hand or machine quilt as desired.

4. Prepare and sew the 2½"-wide binding strips to the quilt.

Finishing Your Quilt

This section contains the information you'll need to finish your quilt, from squaring up blocks through signing and dating your work. Be sure to take a look at the pieced backing ideas on page 86.

Squaring Up Blocks

Some quiltmakers trim or square up their blocks before they assemble the quilt top. If you trim, be sure to leave ¼"-wide seam allowances beyond any points or other important block details that fall at the outside edges of the block.

If your blocks become distorted during the stitching process, square them up with a freezer-paper guide. Use an accurate cutting square and a pencil or permanent pen to draw a square (finished block size plus seam allowance) on the plain side of the freezer paper. Iron the freezer paper to your ironing-board cover, plastic-coated side down.

Align the block edges with the penciled lines and pin the block in place. Press with an up-and-down motion, using plenty of heat and/or steam. Let each block cool before you unpin it from the freezer-paper guide.

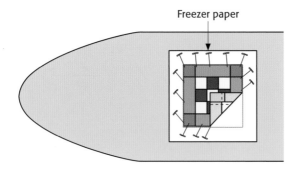

Freezer paper

Adding the Borders

To ensure a flat, straight quilt, always take the border measurements across the center of the patterned section of the quilt, as described more fully below. This guarantees that the borders are of equal lengths on opposing sides of the quilt and brings the outer edges in line with the center dimension if discrepancies exist. Differences between the cut border strips and the outer edges of the quilt can be eased when the borders are joined to the quilt.

The bordered quilts in this book use one of three common border treatments, as shown and described below.

Straight-cut corners   Corner squares   Mitered corners

Borders with Straight-Cut Corners

To make borders with straight-cut corners, measure the length of the patterned section of the quilt at the center, from raw edge to raw edge. Cut two border strips to that measurement and join them to the sides of the quilt with a ¼"-wide seam, matching the ends and centers and easing the edges to fit.

Now, measure the width of the quilt at the center from edge to edge, including the border pieces you just added. Cut two border strips to that measurement and join them to the top and bottom of the quilt, matching ends and centers and easing as necessary.

Borders with Corner Squares

To make borders with corner squares, measure the length and width of the patterned section of the quilt at the center, from raw edge to raw edge. Cut two border strips to the lengthwise measurement and join them to the sides of the quilt with a ¼"-wide seam, matching the ends and centers and easing the edges to fit.

Now, cut two border strips to the original crosswise measurement, join corner squares to the ends of the strips, and stitch these units to the top and bottom of the quilt, matching ends, seams, and centers, and easing as necessary.

Borders with Mitered Corners

To make borders with mitered corners, first estimate the finished outside dimensions of your quilt including borders. Cut border strips to this length plus at least ½" for seam allowances; it's safer to add 2" to 3" to give yourself some leeway. If your quilt is to have multiple mitered borders, sew the individual strips together and treat the resulting unit as a single piece for mitering.

Mark the centers of the quilt edges and the centers of the border strips with pins. Stitch all four border strips to the quilt with ¼"-wide seams, matching the centers. The border strips should extend the same distance at each end of the quilt. Start and stop your stitching ¼" from the corners of the quilt. Press the seams toward the borders.

Quilt top

Lay the first corner to be mitered on the ironing board, pinning as necessary to keep the quilt from pulling and the corner from slipping. Fold one of the border strips or units under at a 45° angle. Work with the fold until any seams or stripes meet properly; pin at the fold, then check to see that the outside corner is square and that there is no extra fullness at the edges. When everything is flat and square, press the fold.

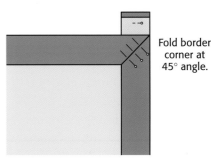

Fold border corner at 45° angle.

Starting at the outside edge of the quilt, center a piece of 1"-wide masking tape over the mitered fold. Remove pins as you apply the tape.

Remove the quilt from the ironing board and turn it over. Draw a light pencil line on the crease created when you pressed the fold. Fold the center section of the quilt diagonally from the corner, right sides together, and align the long edges of the border strips. Stitch on the pencil line, and then remove the tape. Trim the excess fabric and press the seam open. Repeat these steps for the remaining three corners.

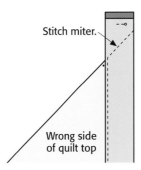

Stitch miter.

Wrong side of quilt top

Preparing the Backing

The backing should be at least 6" wider and 6" longer than the quilt top. For the quilts in this book, plain backings are made by joining three lengths of fabric with ½" seams. Trim off the selvages before you stitch; press the seams open. You can orient the seams either lengthwise or crosswise of the quilt.

If you purchase 108"-wide cotton backing or combine two or more fabrics to piece a strippy-style back, you can use the quilt either side up.

For more variety, or simply to be more frugal, piece a multifabric backing. Use fabric and blocks left over from piecing the front of the quilt; add other fabrics and leftovers from your stash. Quilters have even been known to use quilt tops they're not particularly proud of to back quilts they like better!

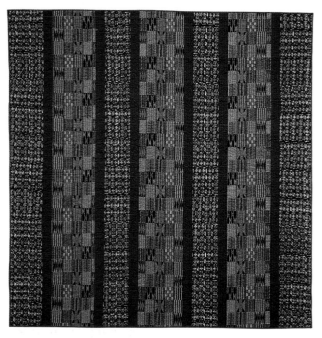

Back of "String Cross," page 78

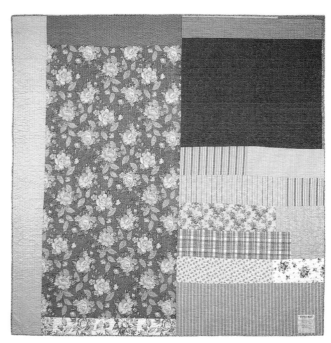

Back of "Quartered Log Cabin," page 75

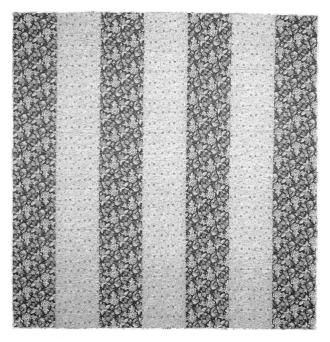

Back of "Progressions," page 71

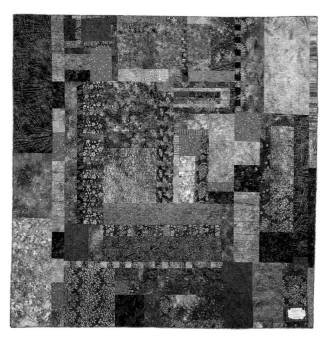

Back of "McKinley Moods," page 60

Preparing to Quilt

Professional quilters using long-arm quilting machines quilted most of the projects in this book. If you opt to have your quilt professionally quilted, check with your long-arm quilter before you deliver your quilt, backing, and batting—quilts don't need to be layered and basted for long-arm machine quilting, but there may be other special requirements you should be aware of.

Follow the instructions in this section if you plan to quilt by hand or on your home sewing machine.

1. Let your batting relax overnight—or toss it in the dryer and let it air-fluff for 10 minutes—before you layer your quilt.

2. Spread the backing on a large table, wrong side up, and anchor it with masking tape or binder clips. Center the batting over the backing, smoothing out any wrinkles.

3. Center the quilt top on the batting, right side up; gently smooth any fullness to the sides and corners. Keep the major horizontal and vertical seams, such as those that attach the borders to the quilt, as straight as possible.

4. For hand quilting, baste the three layers together with a long needle and light-colored thread; start in the center and work diagonally to each corner, making a large X. Continue basting, making a grid of horizontal and vertical lines no more than 6" apart. Finish by basting around the outside edges.

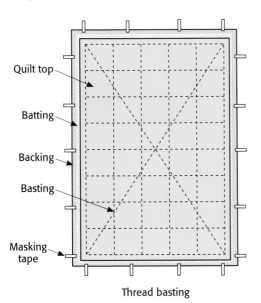

Quilt top
Batting
Backing
Basting
Masking tape

Thread basting

For machine quilting, baste the layers with No. 2 rustproof safety pins placed 3" to 4" apart. Secure the outside edges with straight pins.

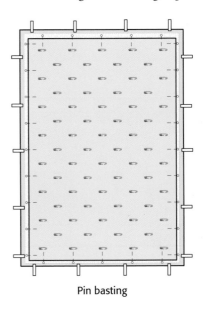

Pin basting

A quilt-tack tool can be used to baste quilts for either hand or machine quilting. The method is fast and holds the layers securely. The T-shaped tabs of the tacks are easy to remove if they get in the way of the needle.

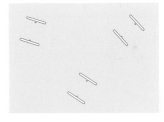

Quilt tacks

Trimming and Straightening the Quilt

When the quilting is complete, remove the basting, except for the stitches around the outside edges of the quilt. (If these stitches are visible, they can be removed after binding.) Measure from a border seam line (or from a major interior seam) to the outside edge of the quilt top in several places around the quilt. Using the smallest measurement, position a ruler along the seam line you measured from and trim the excess batting and backing from all four sides of the quilt. Use a large square ruler to square up the corners.

Adding the Binding

In this book, fabric requirements for bindings assume ⅜"-wide (finished), double-fold binding, made from straight-grain strips cut 2½" wide and stitched to the outside edges of the quilt with a ⅜"-wide seam. You'll need enough binding to go around the perimeter of the quilt plus about 18". Remove the selvages from the binding strips and join the ends to make one long, continuous strip. Press the seams open, then press the strip in half lengthwise, wrong sides together.

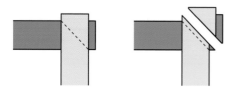

Joining straight-cut strips

Place the binding on the front of the quilt about 15" from a corner, lining up the raw edges of the binding with the raw edges of the quilt. Using a walking foot, sew the binding to the quilt with a ⅜"-wide seam; leave the first 6" of binding loose so you can more easily join the beginning and the end of the binding strip later.

Be careful not to stretch the quilt or the binding as you sew. End the line of stitching ⅜" from the corner of the quilt; backstitch. Remove the quilt from the machine and clip the threads.

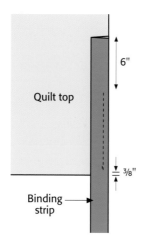

Turn the quilt to prepare for sewing along the next edge. Fold the binding strip away from the quilt at a 45° angle, then fold it back on itself, keeping the raw edge even with the next edge of the quilt. There will be an angled fold at the corner; the second, straight fold should be even with the top edge of the quilt. Beginning ⅜" from the edge of the straight fold, stitch to ⅜" from the next corner, keeping the binding aligned with the raw edge of the quilt.

Fold the binding as you did at the previous corner and continue around the edge of the quilt, repeating the same procedure at the remaining corners.

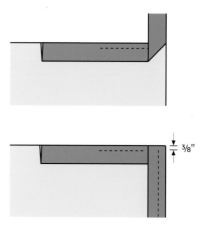

Approximately 10" from the starting point, stop and backstitch. Leave a 6" tail.

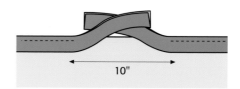

Fold the unstitched binding edges back on themselves so they meet in the middle over the unsewn area of the quilt edge. Press the folds.

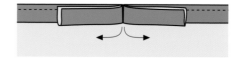

Unfold both ends of the binding. Lay the ending strip flat, right side up. Lay the beginning strip over it, right side down, matching the centers of the pressed Xs. Carefully draw a diagonal line through the point where the fold lines meet. Pin, then stitch on the marked line.

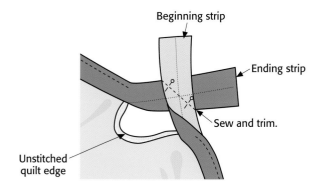

Check to make sure the newly seamed binding fits the unbound edge. Trim off the tail ends ¼" from the seam; press the seam open. Refold the binding, press the fold, and stitch the remainder of the binding to the quilt edge.

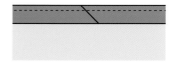

Fold the binding to the back over the raw edges of the quilt. The folded edge of the binding should just cover the stitching line. Blindstitch the binding in place, making sure your stitches don't go through to the front of the quilt. Blindstitch the folds in the miters that form at each corner, if you wish.

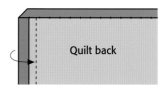

Labeling Your Quilt

Be sure to sign and date your work! At the very least, embroider your name and the year you completed the quilt on the front or back of the quilt. One quilter I know uses her sewing machine's alphabet and number functions to stitch her name and the date on short lengths of grosgrain ribbon. She places these little labels at an angle on the bottom back corners of the quilt and secures the ends when she whips down the binding.

Future generations will want to know more than just the "who" and "when." With today's tools, it's easy to make an attractive and informative label to blindstitch to the back of your quilt. Include the name of the quilt, the maker's name, the quilter's name (if different from the maker), the city and state in which the quilt was made, the date, whom the quilt was made for and why, and any other interesting or important information about the quilt. For an antique quilt, record everything you know about the quilt, including where you purchased it.

Label from "Basket Weave," page 21, created with quilt-label software and printed with an inkjet printer on a commercially available printable fabric sheet

Always test to be absolutely sure the ink used for your label is permanent. Be aware that labels that safely pass the washing-machine test sometimes bleed when they're dry-cleaned. Both handwritten and printed labels may fade with time or after repeated washings.

Making Pillowcases and Shams

I plan my bed quilts without pillow tucks—the top of each quilt just reaches the headboard—and complete the look with coordinating pillowcases or shams. This section contains instructions for making useful accessories for your quilts.

Plain Pillowcases

Two standard size (20" x 31") or two queen size (20" x 35")

You'll need 2½ yards of fabric at least 40" wide for each pair.

For standard pillowcases, cut:
- 2 rectangles, 41" x 36". Fold each in half, right sides together, to make two rectangles, 20½" x 36".

For queen pillowcases, cut:
- 2 rectangles, 41" x 40". Fold each in half, right sides together, to make two rectangles, 20½" x 40".

Assembly

Use ¼" seams.

1. Starting at the fold, seam one short edge and one long edge of each rectangle.
2. Double stitch, or finish the seam with a zigzag or overcast stitch.
3. Turn the open ends under ¼", then 4". Topstitch.

Cuffed Pillowcases

Two queen size

You'll need fabrics at least 40" wide:

1⅞ yards of main fabric

⅞ yard of coordinating fabric for cuffs

⅛ yard of fabric for accent

Measure the width of each fabric and trim the selvage edges as necessary to make all three pieces the same width.

From the main fabric, cut:
- 2 pieces, 29¾" x width of fabric

From the cuff fabric, cut:
- 2 pieces, 13" x width of fabric

From the accent fabric, cut:
- 2 strips, 2" x width of fabric

Assembly

Use ¼" seams except as noted.

1. With right sides together, stitch the short ends of each cuff. Repeat with the accent fabric strips. Press the seams open.
2. Fold the cuff fabric wrong sides together, matching the raw edges. Press the fold. Repeat with the accent fabric.
3. Join the accent fabric to the cuffs with a ¼" seam, matching the raw edges and seams. Double stitch, or finish the seams with a zigzag or overcast stitch.
4. Starting at the fold, seam one short edge and one long edge of the rectangles of the main fabric. Double stitch or finish the seams with zigzag or overcast stitching.
5. With right sides together and the accent fabric next to the main fabric, pin the cuff units to the pillowcases, matching the seams.
6. Join the cuff units to the pillowcases with a ½" seam. Finish the seam, if desired.
7. Turn the pillowcases right side out; press the seams toward the pillowcases. Topstitch through the seams.

Pillow Shams

Two queen size

You'll need fabrics at least 40" wide:

3 yards of main fabric

1 yard of contrasting fabric

From the main fabric, cut:
- 2 rectangles, 21" x 31", for fronts
- 4 rectangles, 20" x 27", for backs

From the contrasting fabric, cut:
- 4 strips, 4" x 31"
- 4 strips, 4" x 27"

Assembly

Use ½" seams.

1. For the fronts, sew the contrasting strips to the 21" x 31" rectangles, long edges first.

2. For the backs, hem a 27" edge of each of the 20" x 27" rectangles by turning the edges under ½" twice; topstitch. Overlap the hemmed edges, forming two rectangles the same size as the fronts; pin.

3. Join the backs to the fronts with a ½" seam, right sides together; turn and press.

4. Topstitch along the edge of the main fabric.

Pillow Covers

A pillow cover is simply a long, narrow quilt that can be draped over or tucked around regular bed pillows. The one pictured below, made to match the "Waterfalls" quilt, measures 35" x 90".

"Waterfalls" pillow cover

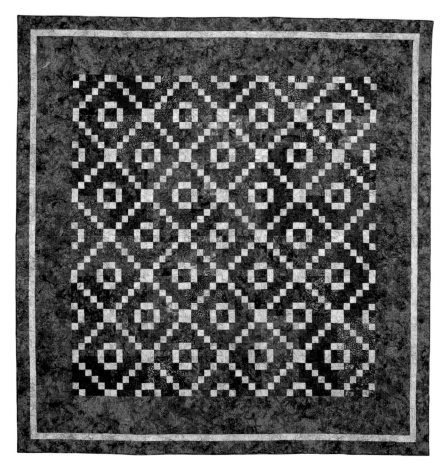

"Waterfalls" quilt

I asked our talented quiltmakers to tell you a little about themselves—probably a more daunting assignment than making a really big quilt (or two). I know you'll enjoy getting acquainted with these interesting, creative women, without whom there would be no book!

Clare Brooks

Juneau, Alaska

"Blocks in a Box," page 24

As a youth, I imagined "quilts" of colorful geometric designs before falling asleep at night. Later, as a working mother of three young children, I kept a scrapbook of quilt pictures from magazines and catalogs. Envisioning beautiful quilts is still a joy even though there still isn't enough time to make them all. For the quilt "Blocks in a Box" pictured in this book, I visualized a delicate flower garden to brighten the dark Alaska winter evenings I spent piecing the blocks. I enjoy the inspirational companionship of quilt-guild members, and the sharing experience of piecing a quilt together through the mail with my talented mother-in-law, Jeanette. I quilt with coworkers during lunch hours, and I especially enjoy consulting with one particularly artistic coworker who helps me pick fabrics.

Rianne Campbell

Anchorage, Alaska

"String Cross," page 78

I'm 13 years old and in the 9th grade at South Anchorage High School. I enjoy reading, skiing, hanging out with friends, and singing. I like to help my mom with her sewing projects, and sometimes I lend a hand with one of Grandma Hopkins's quilts.

Jacquelin Carley

Anchorage, Alaska

"Ladders," page 57

Since I started quilting in 1983, my style has undergone a lot of changes. I started out doing everything by hand, making very traditional quilts using just one or two colors. In the mid '80s I started making scrap quilts, still very traditional. By the mid '90s I was experimenting more and more with color and shape and began making large wall quilts, rather than bed quilts. By the end of the '90s, I was cutting shapes freehand and designing smaller wall quilts with no preconceived idea of the finished product. My current quilts average about 24" x 18" and often feature several different techniques, such as machine reverse appliqué, raw-edge machine appliqué, collage, thread painting, computer-generated images, and machine quilting.

Judy DeLano

Beaverton, Oregon

"Nine Patch Strippy," page 68

My mother taught me to use a sewing machine when I was nine years old. I made my first pieced quilt 30 years ago using cardboard patterns. Since retiring from a career in banking, I've mastered the rotary cutter and have made countless quilts for family and friends. I think the best thing about making a quilt for someone is that you think about that person the entire time you are planning, cutting, and sewing the quilt.

Janet Strait Gorton
Anchorage, Alaska
"Cornucopia," page 31

I've lived in Alaska for almost 40 years and am fortunate to have an understanding husband and two sons who have spent the last 20 years stepping over fabric to get to the kitchen! But besides my two (so far) terrific grandchildren, I don't think anything can compare to the camaraderie and the friendships you can make while quilting.

Michele A. Hall
Aloha, Oregon
"Far West," page 45,
and "Millennium," page 64

I have a background in art, mechanical drafting, and technical writing. My two biggest passions are quilting and dogs. I started quilting in the early 1990s, but didn't do much until 1998. After numerous traditional techniques and quilts, I'm exploring crazy quilts, art quilts, and embellishment. From 1999 through 2003, I raised eight puppies for Guide Dogs for the Blind with my husband, Jeff, and was a leader for our local puppy club. We have three pet dogs—Dasha, a golden retriever; Sailor, a smooth collie; and Gryphon, also a smooth collie. I do agility and rally obedience with our dogs, as well as therapy work through Delta Society.

Sarah Kaufman
Haleiwa, Hawaii
"Checkers," page 34

I met author Judy in the 8th grade at Fifth Street School in Juneau, Alaska—several years before Alaska became a state. We were buddies in home ec class, sewed jumpers together, and double-dated. All these years later the friendship continues: we quilt, talk quilting, and attend quilt shows together. My passion over the past decade or two has been folded-log-cabin quilting. What a pleasure it has been to depart from that style for a while, to make a queen-size quilt for Judy's latest book.

Julie Wilkinson Kimberlin
Temecula, California
"McKinley Moods," page 60

I'm a self-taught needle artist who began sewing at age 13. (I'm still using the same machine.) I love color. I graduated from the University of Washington in 1971 with a BA in Textiles, Clothing, and Art. While I've never used my specialty, the learning never ends. I began what I thought was a "granny thing"— quilting—in 1985. I'm not sure what triggered the interest that became the disease. My credits include two national ribbons and having my work published 22 times. This is my fourth quilt for a "Judy book," and I've quilted several others in her books for other quiltmakers. I've been married for 25 years; my daughter is currently attending the University of Washington.

Martha M. Morris
Juneau, Alaska
"Waterfalls," page 81

I've sewn all my life; when my youngest left for college I gave myself permission to quilt during "prime time," not just the few moments squeezed in around "real" life. I love playing with color and finding what looks good together, with both the right and left brain doing the work. Then comes the fun of cutting and piecing and finally watching the pattern and interaction appear. There are always surprises along the way.

We live on the edge of Auke Bay with ocean ahead and forest behind. That brings me joy as I quilt and gaze out the window. My other source of joy is my family, especially my grandchildren who all sew with me, selecting fabric and creating designs. And what would we do without quilting friends?

Kathy Mosher

Anchorage, Alaska

"**Bars**," page 19

I've made Alaska my home for the past 32 years, with my husband, Kip, and my children, Jennifer and Patrick. In addition to working full-time for the federal government, I have a long-arm quilting business and teach part-time at local quilt shops. The oldest of six children, I started as a seamstress when I was 14, out of necessity! Since that time, quilting has become my passion, especially hand appliqué and quilting. After work at my "real" job, my best stress-reliever is to scour the local shops and stroke bolts of fabric (and buy, of course!). My buying is reflected in the 95 boxes of fabric I claim are waiting for my retirement.

Nellie Oldaker

Juneau, Alaska

"**Courthouse Stars**," page 37

When my daughters were young I sewed garments. Then I didn't sew at all for many years. After my children were grown and living in other states with families of their own, I wanted to sew again to fill some empty hours. I bought a new sewing machine and started quilting. Now my days are full of quilting friends and activities, and my house is full of sewing machines and fabric. Life is good!

Carol Parks

Beaverton, Oregon

"**Burgoyne Surrounded**," page 26

I became interested in quilting after I received a table runner as a Christmas gift from my parents. I took my first quilt class in the spring of 1997 and was instantly hooked. After seeing my first long-arm quilting machine, I came home and told my husband "I will have one!" My machine was delivered in 2000 and I was off and quilting. Since then I've enjoyed having my own business, quilting for myself and for others.

Terri Shinn

Snohomish, Washington

"**Quartered Log Cabin**," page 75

I've been quilting for more than 30 years. My work has been honored with many awards and has been published in numerous books and magazines. I was chosen as "Artist of the Year 2005" for Snohomish County in Washington State. Even though I continue to experiment with mixed media, I still enjoy doing traditional quilts. Probably the most unusual item on my resume is that I once made a series of quilts from fabric painted by an elephant.

Juanita Stark

Eugene, Oregon

"**Grandmother's Choice**," page 53

I fell in love with quilting about 12 years ago when I walked into a quilt shop and saw all the beautiful quilts hanging on the walls. Now I spend as much time as possible in my quilt room making quilts. Sometimes I think my fabric stash is taking over the room! I have a lot of help from my cat, Sophie, who likes to get right in the middle of whatever project I'm working on. I enjoy pieced blocks and I love hand appliqué. I have a son and daughter, five grandchildren, and one great-grandson. I've taught my daughter and her best friend how to quilt, and recently taught one of my granddaughters.

Kathy White

Aloha, Oregon

"**Basket Weave**," page 21

I took my first quilting stitches in 1967, helping my mother hand quilt a quilt for my soon-to-be-born daughter, and I've been at it ever since. For several years my passion for quilting had to take a back seat to my need for garment sewing, but no more. As a teacher of quilting I share in the excitement of my students as they discover the marvels of the world of quilting. Quilting satisfies both my need to be creative and my desire to do something for others, as the majority of my quilts are made for someone else.

About the Author

Judy Hopkins comes from a family of quilters: her grandmother, her mother, and her aunt all made quilts. She started pursuing a full-time career in quilting after being named Alaska's state winner of the Great American Quilt Contest (the "Liberty Contest") in 1986.

Judy is the author of 15 design and pattern books for quilters, including the three-volume *Around the Block* series and *101 Fabulous Rotary-Cut Quilts* (with Nancy J. Martin). Her love of scrap-bag quilts, old and new, led to the design of her popular ScrapMaster ruler, a tool for quick-cutting half-square triangles from irregularly shaped scraps.

Judy has specialized in mystery quilt patterns since the early 1990s; she writes a mystery series for *Quilting Professional* magazine and produces a line of mystery quilt patterns for individual quilters—Mystery Quilt Singles—in partnership with Marsha McCloskey of Feathered Star Productions.

Judy lives in Juneau, Alaska, with her husband, Bill. She has five adorable and brilliant grandchildren who like to help her sew. Without granddaughter Rianne Campbell's strip-sewing skills, the quilt "String Cross" on page 78 might never have been completed!